THE UNFLUSHABLES
OUTHOUSES–HISTORY AND HUMOR

Rachel & Jim,

This was given to us by our friend, Mark Weber, whose grandfather wrote this book! ☺ His grandma is the one on the balcony of the front cover photo. When I told Mark I had a dear friend whose powder room is outhouse-themed, he said, "You have to give her this book!" And I'm sure Mr. History (aka Jim) will enjoy this as well!!

☺ With love at Christmastime,
♡ Heather & Dan

Also by Walter Weber

Signs of Your Life

Funny Bones: Health and Humor Experts (co-author)

Health Hazards from Pigeons, Starlings and English Sparrows

Diseases Transmitted by Rats and Mice

Fleas, Ticks & Cockroaches, Disease Disseminators

THE UNFLUSHABLES
OUTHOUSES–HISTORY AND HUMOR

Featuring Two-, Three-, and Five-Story Outhouses

Helping Preserve One Slice of American History
and Specialized Architecture

WALTER J. WEBER

Copyright © 1989 by Walter J. Weber.

All rights reserved. No part of this publication may be reproduced or used in any form or by any means, stored in a retrieval system, or transmitted by any form or by any means, electronic, mechanical, photographic, recording, or otherwise, without written permission of the publisher, excluding book reviews.

Published by:
Walter J. Weber, 36 West Roberts Road, Indianapolis, IN 46217, (317) 786-7251.

ISBN 0-937959-86-3
Library of Congress Catalog Card No. 89-90346
Printed in U.S.A.

Publishing consultant:
Falcon Press Publishing Co., Inc.
Helena, Montana

This book is dedicated to

(a) Individuals who furnished pictures,
(b) Family members and friends who encouraged publication,
(c) Mary Burns, who enthusiastically typed the manuscript,
(d) Those nice people who bought a copy, and
(e) All of the above.

Contents

Foreword:	Privial Pursuit	11
Introduction:	Privy Preservationists	15
Chapter 1:	Preplumbing Pitless Privies	19
Chapter 2:	Double Deckers	27
Chapter 3:	Triple Deckers	43
Chapter 4:	More Story Outhouses (Four and Five)	49
Chapter 5:	Presidential Thrones	51
Chapter 6:	Historical Outhouses	57
Chapter 7:	Relaxicating Rendezvouses– Reservations Requested	79
Chapter 8:	May I Be Excused?	87
Chapter 9:	Please Be Seated	93
Chapter 10:	Inhouse Outhouses	99
Chapter 11:	Lightening the Load– Posted Privies	107

CHAPTER 12:	HUMOROUS SIGNS OF THE TIMES	115
CHAPTER 13:	PRIVIA TRIVIA	127
CHAPTER 14:	PRIVY PRIVILEGES FOR PAMPERED PETS AND OTHER ANIMALS	133
APPENDIX:		139
ABOUT THE AUTHOR:		141

FOREWORD
PRIVIAL PURSUIT

Not all outhouses were created equal. "Is there really a two-story outhouse?" "I never heard of such a thing!" "How did it work?" "I surely wouldn't want to be the person on the bottom deck!" "Are you kidding?" These comments have been made when I told about seeing my first double decker in Virginia City, Montana. I had never heard of one until I encountered it behind the old hotel. Fortunately, I had my camera with me. This was the beginning of my interest in old outhouses, a relic of yesteryear.

In the days before EPA, computers, television, disposable diapers, toilet tissue, and flush toilets, there were unflushables. They were known as outhouses, privies, and toilets. The names have become synonymous. The word privy is derived from the Latin *privatus*, meaning apart or private. The word toilet is from the French *toilette*, for bathing. About fifty nicknames or euphemisms include back forty, backhouse, bathroom, biffie, cabana, camp jon, can, chamber, chic sale, comfort station, commode, crapper, donniker, deposit box, dooley, dry closet, easey, head, hopper, hospitality house, house of hospitality, house of the morning, house out back, jake, jimmie, jon, jonnie, latrine, lavatory, library, little dooley, little house, little house out back, Mrs. Jones, necessary parlor, place of easement, pot, reading room, restroom, sanitary house, shack, shanty, shed, sitting down place, sugar shack, thinking house, throne room, two seater, wat-ch-M-call-it, water closet, Willie, and many appellations which will not be included in a coffee table book. The common name in Australia is dunny.

The first American outhouses were built by early settlers. The hardships they faced included a lack of food, fending off of hostile people, living in a dangerous environment, and trips to the privy in bitter cold weather. That little old outhouse was of major importance to everyone. At one time the outhouse was standard equipment on all farms and all homes that lacked running water. Except for the house, the privy was probably the most important building on the place. It served its daily purpose in a worthy, respectable, and uncomplicated manner. There was never any doubt about the purpose of one's visit. Outhouses were part of society's progress and served an essential role in the development of America. However, they are rapidly disappearing from our heritage, and they are vanishing from the American landscape. Now they are considered antiques and in some cases are collector's items. Some have been moved to museum grounds.

An outhouse bridges the gap to the past. It represents the days when nearly everyone worked long hours and had few of today's comforts. Now some people yearn for "those good old days." Those people need to realize that folks didn't always live in a push-button, knob-turning world of comfort. Some people just can't imagine life without color television, electricity, and flush toilets.

Outhouses are a short chapter in a very long story. Everybody needed an outhouse: the rich, the poor; the young, the old; the ambitious, the lazy; the happy people, the grouches; the fat people, the skinny ones. There were no class distinctions. All privies served the same purpose: they relieved a situation which confronts the entire population. They provided the pleasant use of spare time with complete relief and satisfaction.

This book is not about today's fiberglass, one-hole, rented outhouses seen at construction sites, sporting events, and public meetings. This book tells the story about some of those old unflushables and preserves a slice of Americana that will soon be nonexistent.

I would like to thank all of the marvelous individuals and organizations for their cooperation. They helped in providing an interesting assortment of pictures and information depicting outdoor specialties. I especially want to acknowledge the patience of my good wife, the help of my two sons, David and Steven, who arranged for converting my slides into prints, my grandchildren for taking some of the pictures and providing suggestions, and for the perserverance of a marvelous secretary, Mary Burns, for correcting and typing the manuscript.

It would be a pleasure to hear from anyone who has information about or pictures of historical or unusual outhouses. I am always interested in additional information for use in my presentation, "If Unflushables Could Talk."

Walter Weber

INTRODUCTION
PRIVY PRESERVATIONISTS

Preservationists and historians are wonderful, thoughtful people who take the mystery out of history. The 1986 edition of *Historical Agencies in North America* lists 9,375 museums and historic, preservation, and similar societies. One example of which I am a member is the Indiana Historical Society with a membership of approximately 6,500.

There is a great deal of value and dignity surrounding the historic unflushables that have been preserved. They served their purpose well and served an essential role in the lives of early settlers and their descendants. Those outhouses represent a remnant of the past which is completely foreign to many people.

Indoor plumbing was a luxury in the 1870s that was available only to the wealthy. Most bathrooms of that day were designed only for bathing. The water was gravity-fed from a large holding tank in the attic. Even though some of the homes had water for bathing, they still used outhouses.

Prediction of the demise of the outhouse was made prior to World War I by poet Charles T. Rankin in his famous poem, "Passing of the Backhouse." You will find it near the end of this book.

Unflushables deserve recording before they become completely extinct. Outhouses were not featured in our school texts or news media. Pioneer journalists dealt with the large issues such as wars, treaties, politics, current events, mansions, and big shots. We need to remember most of history is based on common people. Journalists didn't spend much time writing about common things such as privies. Possibly photographers were prudish sorts who didn't believe that unflushables were appropriate subjects for the new technology of photography, so the opportunities to record evidence of outdoor plumbing were overlooked. Apparently, the people did not think enough of their outhouses to take pictures.

Fortunately, the efforts of historic preservationists have saved not only mansions and remnants of the leaders and wealthy. In some cases, they have included the historic value and dignity of utilitarian structures, including the unflushables. Their thoughtful preservation shows a more comprehensive understanding of history.

We cannot re-live history, but we can review one segment that was very much a part of the eighteenth, nineteenth, and early twentieth centuries. Many people have lost touch with a crucial part of what historical experiences are all about. Many famous people grew up using outhouses, including teachers, preachers, doctors, farmers, inventors, and presidents.

Now privy sites have become places for archaeologists to gather and learn. Historians have extensive records of how the rich and famous lived. The paintings, china, and possessions of the wealthy have been preserved, but the records of the poor often ended in the privy holes.

There is an entirely new vista of early American history unfolding for people who have never used or seen one of those unflushables. One of the questions often asked during tours of historic homes is, "Where's the bathroom?" After noting that people used outhouses, the curator is asked another question, "What's an outhouse?" One man told about taking his granddaughter on a fishing trip. After he had escorted her to the outhouse and she had completed her mission, she asked, "Grandpa, how do you flush it?"

Unflushables appeared in many shapes, styles, and sizes, but every one was functional and had one end in mind—to serve the same personal human need. There was a diverse variety in structures. Some showed originality. Many were simple, others were elaborately decorated with fancy cupolas, gingerbread, and finials. Some had windows, neatly starched lace curtains, attractively papered walls, and nice carpets. Some even had porches. In a few cases, there were gold-plated doorknobs and mirrors on the wall. Occasionally, it was even equipped with a heating stove. Unflushables were often the subject of expert craftsmanship and artistry. Some of the better outhouses had double walls for added warmth.

Convenience and comfort usually depended on the concern and skill of the builder, who had to consider several factors. An outhouse had to be close enough to the house for convenience, but not close enough to create an objectionable aroma in hot weather.

Outhouses were usually kept in good repair, but there have been cases where people were seriously injured as they fell through the seat or floor. A specific example was given by a cousin who formerly lived in Mount Vernon, Ohio. A very plump lady fell through the seat in the half-moon bungalow, and the fire department had to extricate her from the pit.

There aren't too many outhouses in actual use today, but they are very close to the recent past. In many areas, they are considered antiques. It is my desire to share those vanishing relics of early American history and their important services.

Outhouses are real. They represent a specialized type of architecture. These pictures prove it. Photographs have been used wherever available, since people learn more through sight than any of the four other senses. The pictures are from forty-two states, four Canadian provinces, and two foreign countries. I hope you find this photographic journey fascinating, for in these images you can visualize life in earlier years.

CHAPTER 1
PREPLUMBING PITLESS PRIVIES

A bottomless hole, I guess you could say, was quite a popular model with some early settlers. Some outhouses were strategically placed over a stream so that all of the waste would find its way into the flowing waters. In other cases, they were located on docks of harbors and lakes. Some were located on beaches in such a manner that the incoming tides took care of a daily flushing, with all waste going out to sea. Early monasteries and castles in other countries were frequently located so that the sanitary tower extended over the moat.

A Straight Flush in Alaska, the Last Frontier State (49th State, 1959)

This outhouse in Hoonah never had to be cleaned out. Of course, a person had to step lightly and had to walk the straight and narrow path, whether sober or not.

Photo courtesy the Anchorage Museum of History and Art, B75-175-584.

Over the Water in Alaska

This 1938 picture in Klawock, Alaska, shows a mighty convenient privy close to the home from Peratrovich Dock. There was genuine essentiality and practicability in this little indispensable structure before the days of EPA and before Alaska became a state. It was in 1857 when Alaska was purchased from Russia for $7,200,000, which was less than two cents per acre.

Photo courtesy the Anchorage Museum of History and Art, B75-175-630.

Natural Flush in Idaho, the Gem of the Mountains State (43rd State, 1890)

This privy hangs precariously over the edge of the Boise River, and waste fell directly into the river. According to Hugh Hartman, well-known historian, "This one sat at 'Ma Kirk's place' up on the Boise River above Boise, Idaho. Her place is now under the back waters of Lucky Peak Dam. Ma Kirk ran a gas station, store, bar, dance hall, and other services across the river. The homestead also went across the river, where they grew fruit and had picnics. They had a cable stretched across the river with a small hand car attached, and this was their mode of fording the river. This outhouse was unique because it had running water. As you sat on the throne on one side, you could look down the other hole and see the running water. You can see the river just to the right of the outhouse through the shrubs." Ma Kirk's has been gone for forty years, but Hartman says he can still remember the sound of the river flowing below as he did his business.

Photo courtesy Hugh Hartman, Idaho historian.

A Creek Straddler in Idaho

This Masonic hall in Silver City was originally a wood-milling shop built across Jordan Creek. The two outhouses attached to the hall dropped deposits directly into the stream below. Later a city ordinance prohibited their use except during flood stage.

Photo copyright 1988 by Norman D. Weis, from The Two Story Outhouse, *Caxton Printers, Ltd. See Appendix.*

Privy-Bridge Combo in Idaho

This trestle job in Burke provided automatic flushing as Canyon Creek carried away all of its deposits. Gold was first discovered in the area in 1860. This could be the only outhouse-bridge in existence. One could well assume that it was used by more than one family, none of whom were exactly ardent environmentalists.

Photo copyright 1988 by Norman D. Weis, from The Two Story Outhouse, *Caxton Printers, Ltd. See Appendix.*

Up the Creek in Indiana, the Hoosier State
(19th State, 1816)

This privy, part of a tavern, emptied directly into the creek in Weisberg, Indiana. The Weisburg Brauhaus was built in 1903, and there was no concern about having to clean out the privy. The Board of Health put a stop to its use in 1955. This information was provided by a lifetime resident, Joe Rosemeyer, who celebrated his 100th birthday September 4, 1988. He told me that two of the three taverns in Weisburg solved their privy problems by the use of this creek. Weisburg was one of the areas visited by the Morgan Raiders during the Civil War.

Mrs. William Innis, West Palm Beach, Florida, was the first person to tell me about the pitless privy which is only about an hour's distance from my house. Mrs. Innis was born close to the

area where Weisburg is located. She told how her great-great-grandmother was baking bread when one of the Morgan Raiders stopped at her home and politely explained that he would have to take the freshly baked bread for the men in that group of the Union Army.

Photo by Walter Weber

Creek-Drop Attached Privy in Idaho

You didn't wear out your legs going to this handy house built over Canyon Creek in Burke, and no one knew what you wore that morning. This gold miner's overhanger was probably built in the 1890s.

Photo copyright 1988 by Norman D. Weis, from The Two Story Outhouse, *Caxton Printers, Ltd. See Appendix.*

Almost Self-Flushing in British Columbia, Canada

Some people settled near a source of running water. This attached privy in Sandon, British Columbia, emptied directly into Carpenter Creek. Buckets of privy waste and dirty sink water were dumped directly into the creek, where they were carried downstream through the town far below. The town of Sandon was built along both sides of Carpenter Creek. The melting snows destroyed many buildings, but this one was spared by a rocky bank, which deflected the waters.

Photo courtesy Lambert Florin, author of Backyard Classics.

Over the Bayou in Louisiana, the Pelican State (18th State, 1812)

Running water is included. One cannot view this privy without thinking about sparkling sunbeams playing upon the tiny ripples and maybe some alligators. This picture was taken before the days of instant coffee.

Photo courtesy of the Louisiana State Museum.

Reminiscent Reflection in Maine, the Pine Tree State (23rd State, 1820)

It looks out of focus, but this picture was taken from a boat in 1864, when photography was still a recent development. The first daguerreotype was produced in 1839. The first sunlight picture of a human face was made in New York in 1840. The earliest-known American spot news photograph was made by George Barnard in Oswego, New York, in 1847. Now look at the reflection of the outhouse sitting on the wharf in Yarmouth harbor. You can see the reflection of a round circle as evidence that everything went directly into the water below.

Photo courtesy Yarmouth (Maine) Historical Society.

CHAPTER 2
DOUBLE DECKERS

Would you be surprised to see a two-story outhouse when you had never even heard that such a structure existed? My first lesson in two stories was in 1963. Fortunately, I had my camera.

The normal question is "How did it work?" The rear wall of the downstairs section of a two-story outhouse is not the back of the building. The top-deck seat bench is located all the way back. The offset walls form a chute down the back wall so that the waste can collect below. This chute protected the occupant of the lower story from an unpleasant surprise. Two-story outhouses were occasionally connected to homes, but were usually associated with rooming houses, hotels, dance halls, and saloons. In places where the snow reached depths of six to twelve feet, they were almost a necessity.

My First Double Decker in Montana, the Treasure State (41st State, 1889)

I had never heard of a two-story outhouse until I saw this one in Virginia City, Montana, the second territorial capital from 1856 to 1875. Robbers Roost is a short distance down the road. The caretaker will explain that people who robbed stagecoaches and others were known as "road runners." He will point out the bullet holes in the wall and tell how Henry Plummer, a convicted criminal, became marshal and appointed two of his fellow road runners as deputies. The trio maintained law and order during the day and robbed at night until the vigilantes caught up with them. He will also show you a photo of the three suspended from the gallows. The last stagecoach robbery was in 1892 by a woman.

Photo by Walter Weber.

Second Floor, Please, in Montana

How did a two story work? Is that your question? This two story is from Townsend, Montana. It was built in the days when a chip meant a piece of wood, and hardware meant hard wear and software wasn't even a word.

The deadliest vigilante movement occurred in Montana in 1864 when thirty-five accused thieves and murderers were hanged.

Photo courtesy the Montana Historical Society.

A Tall Two Story in Nevada, the Silver State (36th State, 1864)

This two story served the guests of a hotel in Dayton, Nevada. If you look at those two open doors on the top level, you could logically conclude that it must have provided accommodations for about three people in each section at one time. It was still standing in 1976, but is gone now.

Photo courtesy the Nevada Historical Society.

Two Up and Four Down in Calgary, Alberta, Canada

This impressive double decker was originally located in Lundbreck, Alberta. Built in 1905, it was connected by a catwalk to the Windsor Hotel so that the second-story guests could have quick access. The outhouse (left) was all that survived the fire when the hotel burned to the ground in 1963. The outhouse was donated to and moved to beautiful Heritage Park (right) in 1965.

Photo courtesy Heritage Park.

Double Decker in Illinois, the Prairie State (21st State, 1818)

This two-story four holer in Gays was built about 1872 by F. S. Gammell after he returned from the Civil War. He built a general store with his own residence and several apartments on the second floor. (That was in the days before frozen foods and pizza.) The privy is about ten feet behind the store, with the top floor connected by a walkway. It was a long walk to go down the stairs and down the path every time nature called, so he built a double decker. The upper floor seats were on the west side, the lower floor seats on the east side. It is said that no Halloween pranksters have ever successfully toppled it. Townspeople are so proud of their double decker that they built a replica of it for use in the Fourth of July celebration. It was once featured in *Ripley's Believe It or Not.*

Photo by Walter Weber.

Two-Story Attached in Illinois

This historic vertican in Galena shows that convenience must have had top priority. It is attached to the porch of the Bradner Smith "Half House," built in 1855. The builder had originally planned to build the other half at a later date.

Access to the upper level of the vertican is from the upper level of the two-story porch (behind the lattice). Access to the lower level is from the porch adjacent to the kitchen at ground level. All the indications show that the privy was probably built at the time the house was constructed. My friend, Richard Vincent, and the owner, Richard Clark, showed me where the food was prepared in the old kitchen in the basement. The food and dinnerware were elevated to the second floor using a dumbwaiter, which is still seen in the old kitchen.

The house had conventional inside plumbing when Dick

Clark bought it in 1961, but he was amazed to discover that instead of being attached to a city sewer, the soil stack simply ran into the old outhouse pit. So, in an unsavory sense, he may have had the most recently used two-story outhouse.

The upper level is intact with two well-worn adult holes and one smaller child-size hole in a lower bench. Fortunately, this gem of history has been retained intact, except that the lower level has been converted to tool storage. Galena also had a four- and five-story outhouse as explained in Chapter Four.

Photo and information courtesy Richard Vincent.

Clinging Bi-Level in California, the Golden State (31st State, 1850)

This tall two story clings to the side of an old hotel in Sierra City, near the north end of California's gold chain of mining camps. This outhouse was a self-cleaner, as the creek carried waste into the Yuba River at the bottom of the hill. Towering cliffs directly above town often allowed destructive avalanches.

Photo courtesy Lambert Florin, author of Backyard Classics.

Is This a Jontower? In Michigan, the Wolverine State
(26th State, 1837)

One name for an outhouse is jon. It has been said that an outhouse stacked on top of another outhouse could be called a jontower. I wouldn't want to be the fellow using the bottom floor. This two story stood all by itself in Edmore, located in upper Michigan. There was no evidence of an old hotel or other adjoining building.

Photo courtesy State Archives of Michigan, Neg. No. 01180.

Immediate Convenience in North Dakota, the Flickerbird State
(39th State, 1889)

This double decker was one mile south of Alfred, North Dakota. The picture and information were kindly provided by Barbara Hird of Edgeley. She visited 97-year-old Mr. Henne in a retirement home on September 3, 1988. Mr. Henne explained that the original fourteen-room house was built with rocks by a Mr. Sykes before the railroad came in (around 1900). The walls of the house were about two feet thick. The wood frame addition with the double decker was built on later by Mr. Sykes. Mr. Henne said the two-story outhouse was still there when he went to the army in 1917, but was gone when he returned from the service in 1919. Mr. Henne later lived in the house.

Forrest Daniel, formerly with the North Dakota Historical Society, tells about a two-story outhouse that at one time was attached to a hotel in Dawson, North Dakota. It used to be an attraction for people traveling east on the train.

Photo and information courtesy Barbara Hird, Edgeley Centennial book chairperson, and Max Hird, Centennial book photographer.

Top-Floor Convenience in Minnesota, the Gopher State (32nd State, 1858)

A family of fourteen lived in this house. The eleven daughters were probably happy their father solved their concern for going from a nice warm house into a cold outhouse with the enclosed walkway to the second floor of this two-story gem. This house, belonging to the Belle Plaine Historical Society, is considered the most photographed house in Belle Plaine. The six holer dates back to 1886. Some outhouses had a hinged flap door that permitted easy access for cleaning.

Photo courtesy Belle Plaine Historical Society.

A Grafted-On Two Story in Colorado, the Centennial State (38th State, 1876)

The front side of Crested Butte, Colorado's, town hall is a beautiful structure. If you examine the building, you will find this two-story privy, which seems to be grafted on to the back side. The outhouse for all seasons.

Photo copyright 1988 by Norman D. Weis, from The Two Story Outhouse, *Caxton Printers, Ltd. See Appendix.*

Two-Story Annex in Colorado

The snow may reach eight or nine feet in Crested Butte, but this second story can be reached by a catwalk from the second floor of the Masonic lodge or from the covered stairway. Crested Butte was first established as a coal mining area, but now it is a famous ski resort. This palace of comfort has delighted many sit-ins.

Photo copyright 1988 by Norman D. Weis, from The Two Story Outhouse, *Caxton Printers, Ltd. See Appendix.*

An Airborne Outhouse in Indianapolis

The earliest anticipated balloon ascension in the United States occurred on January 9, 1793, while President George Washington and a large crowd watched. The earliest unanticipated ascension of an outhouse occurred at the Indianapolis Speedway on May 14, 1966. The unplanned, unprogrammed, unofficial, unscheduled event surprised everybody when the wicker basket of an ascending balloon caught on the corner of an unflushable and carried it about forty feet. This indisputable first airborne unflushable was occupied by two ladies. Could these have been the first lady astronauts?

Information courtesy Bob Laycock, Indianapolis Motor Speedway.

Two-Story Biffie in Indiana

You can't judge a building by its cover. Long ago, this outhouse once stood in an area of Indianapolis that is now the Indiana University Medical Center. This was before the days of penicillin, polio shots, and antibiotics. Indianapolis is the largest city in the United States without a navigable waterway. It is best known as the U.S. racing capital, especially on Memorial Day weekends.

Photo courtesy Ken Beckley and Sandra Hartlieb, Indiana University, Purdue, University of Indianapolis.

Split Level in Wyoming, the Equality State
(44th State, 1890)

Climb the stairs and drop your cares. This well-preserved early bi-level is located in the town of Encampment, near the local museum. It was moved from its original spot in Battle. The sign identifies it as "Early Day High Mountain Outhouse." The deep snow encouraged second-floor usage. This was built before the days of ice makers and freezers.

Photo courtesy Jerry D. Paxton, President, Wyoming Vocational Agriculture Teachers Association.

Watch Out Below in Idaho

This famed two-story uncommon accommodation in Silver City, Idaho, served an illustrious career. This design was probably posteriorly preeminent. They don't make them like they used to. This one could be readily reached from a building that had been used as a mining camp office and hospital. What people did here never made the headlines. There were no fluorescent lights in this one.

Photo courtesy Lambert Florin, author of Backyard Classics.

Walk-Through Two Story in Idaho

This unusual walk-through tall privy stands behind the tin-shop and newspaper office in Silver City. Its closeness to Jordan Creek, which runs under the Masonic lodge just behind, made the annual cleanout almost automatic. In its heyday, Silver City boasted Idaho's first daily newspaper and a population of 5,000 people. By 1920, it had fallen to 100.

Photo and information courtesy Norman D. Weis, from The Two Story Outhouse, *Caxton Printers, Ltd. See Appendix.*

Two Floors for Better Service in Arizona, the Grand Canyon State (48th State, 1912)

The first time we were in Oatman, we saw a big sign on one of the buildings, "Where the West was lost." This picture was hanging in the hotel. There was no label or information on the picture, so its origin is a mystery. No one in the hotel seemed to know where this classic two story was located, and there were no Xerox records then. Oatman was formerly an active gold and silver mining center; in fact, one street was named Payroll. Now the town caters to tourists during winter months.

Photo courtesy Norman D. Weis, from The Two Story Outhouse, *Caxton Printers, Ltd. See Appendix.*

A Two-Story Attached in Germany

This two story is attached to a hotel in Germany. Close observation shows that it is well supported by heavy timbers. Dr. Dieter Strauch, University of Hohenheim in Stuttgart, was doing an extensive research project on hygiene of toilets in airplanes, buses, railways, rest places alongside highways, and camping sites. This is evidence that many people are interested in sanitation, including some early history.

Photo courtesy Professor Dr. Dieter Strauch.

Bach's Brick Outhouse in Germany

Johann Sebastian Bach (1685-1750), the great composer from Leipzig, Germany, had a two-story brick outhouse attached to his home (now a museum in East Germany). Here is your opportunity to see an early two story and to use your camera—then send a picture of it to me.

Information courtesy Brice Tressler.

A Two Story by a Depot in Kentucky, the Bluegrass State (15th State, 1792)

P. W. England of Beech Grove, Indiana, has experienced eighty-five years of history, which includes seeing a two story. He was about eight years old when his parents took him on his first train ride to meet his grandfather in Lexington. He remembers using the old wooden two story that stood next to the old L & N railroad station.

Information courtesy P. W. England.

A Civil War Two Story in Tennessee, the Big Bend State
(16th State, 1796)

It was in March 1862 that the Federal army captured Nashville, the first Confederate capital to fall. A twenty-hole latrine was built on the side yard of the First Presbyterian Church, but it was closed in January 1864. A two-story outhouse was constructed with four holes upstairs and four holes downstairs. The elbows to the drains were made of leather, but the elbows leaked. It did contain a stove for warmth.

Photo and information courtesy James Hoobler and Robert DePriest, Tennessee State Archives.

Two-Story Brick Privy in Wisconsin, the Badger State
(30th State, 1848)

This historic two-story privy is located in Janesville, Wisconsin. It is part of the William Morrison Tallman house built in 1855-1857. The first floor of the privy is entered from the outside, while the second floor is entered from the hallway in the servants' quarters. The privy is complete with three holes and a

chamberpot disposal hole on each floor, shaft, roof-fed flushing system, and a ventilating shaft, all of which are still intact. A private sewer drained waste water and effluent away from the

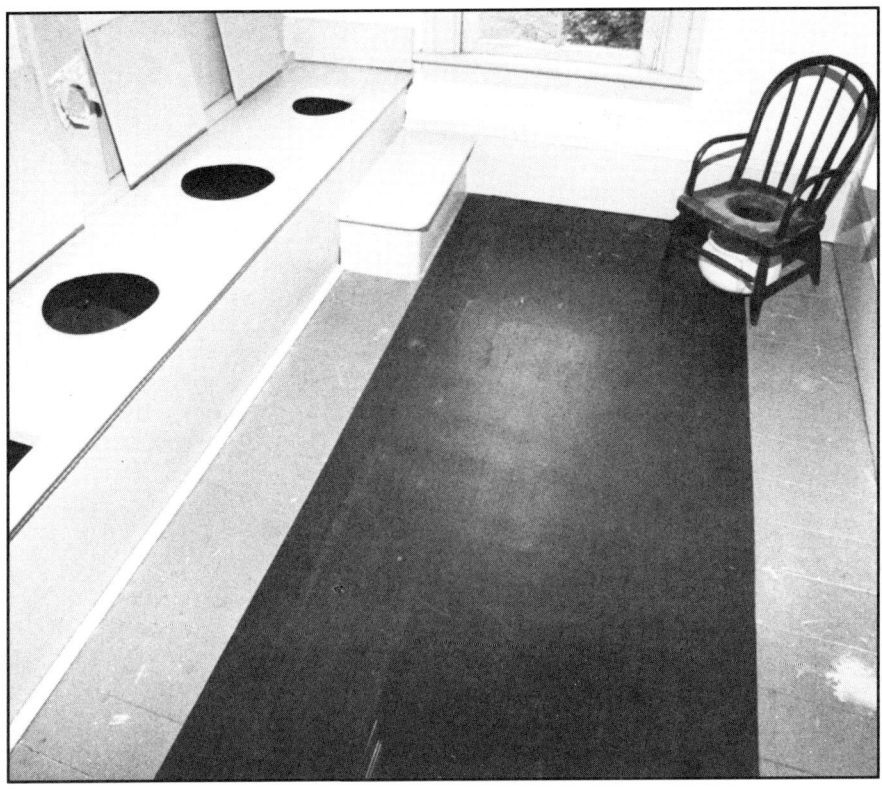

house to the nearby Rock River. The Tallman house is the largest antebellum house in the upper Midwest and is well worth a visit.

Photos courtesy Rock County Historical Society, Janesville, Wisconsin.

CHAPTER 3
TRIPLE DECKERS

So you thought a two-story outhouse couldn't be topped. Here is the evidence that you thought wrong. The triple decker from St. Louis was built in 1870. You can guess the age of the others, and probably no one will argue.

A Three-Way Privy in Colorado

This three-way outhouse is attached to an old saloon in Crested Butte. The top facility serves a dance hall. The second level serves the saloon, while the ground level gives access to the addendum.

Photo courtesy Norman D. Weis, from The Two Story Outhouse, *Caxton Printers, Ltd. See Appendix.*

Triple Decker in Minnesota

A piece of the past in St. Paul, Minnesota, is preserved in this 1940 photo of a three-way privy. It was located a block north of the railroad bridge on State Street. Would this have been a condominium?

Photo by the St. Paul Daily News, *courtesy the Minnesota Historical Society.*

Three Floors Up in Idaho

This is the way things used to be in Silver City, Idaho. It's a reminder of silver mining days. The picture of this three-story outhouse was taken in 1963 before the days of EPA and OSHA. This reliever allowed for discharge of daily duties. Do you think users of the lower levels really took a chance?

Photo courtesy Professor Higgins, University of Idaho.

Three-Story Comfort, St. Louis, Missouri, the Show Me State (24th State, 1821)

This picture taken in 1918 is of a twelve-family, three-story outhouse in St. Louis. Built in 1870, the facility was linked to an apartment building by catwalks. The second and third floors were connected by ingenious shafts to the cesspool below, which unfortunately sometimes filled with methane gas and exploded. In that period, the people who did not have sewers used cesspools, not septic tanks. That was in the days before vitamin pills and decaffeinated coffee.

Information courtesy Tom Murray, author of Passing of the Outhouse; *photo courtesy the Missouri Historical Society, Street Scenes No. 74.*

A Three Story in Nevada

The fourth ward school of Virginia City, Nevada, was completed in 1876 and accommodated more than 1,000 students. It had an outstanding three-story outhouse complex attached. This three-story facility had separate rooms for boys and girls. Access was gained through an outdoor balcony walkway. The outhouse was demolished in the 1950s when it became unstable.

Information courtesy Ronald M. James, Deputy State Historic Preservation Officer; photo courtesy the Nevada Historical Society.

Ben Franklin Had a Three Story in Philadelphia

Benjamin Franklin is remembered for his many achievements. He invented bifocal glasses, and he was responsible for the first fire department and first police department in the colonies, along with the first circulating library. His first public act was to petition Congress for the immediate abolition of slavery. He also owned a three-story house in Philadelphia that had a toilet on every floor. The toilet was in a connected, three-story outhouse. That was in the days before Montgomery Ward catalogs and rolls of toilet tissue. We know that he did own a newspaper. He died in 1790.

CHAPTER 4
MORE STORY OUTHOUSES
(FOUR AND FIVE)

You were not at the peak with the three-story outhouses. How about a four- and five-story privy?

Five Stories, No Elevator, in Illinois

This picture shows the two doors—"his" and "hers"—on the third floor of a famous five-story outhouse in Galena. This lathed and plastered brick privy was built during the 1840s, prior to the Civil War. Its base is twelve feet by fifteen feet, and the top or chimney is eight by eight and fifty feet tall. The steps in the right upper corner are a few of the seventy-five leading to the fifth floor. This outhouse is in the court of a five-story apartment house. The owner has enclosed the court's roof. The outhouse was no longer needed after flush toilets were installed, so the tenants disposed of their ashes by dumping them into the outhouse holes. The rooms are now used for storage. The structure of the apartment building is such that one cannot get a picture of the entire outhouse. There are "his" and "hers" doors on each of the five floors.

An unusual feature in this historic town is the complex of crevices in the underlying limestone, nearly vertical fissures that vary from a fraction of an inch up to six feet in width, from a few feet to more than a mile in length. This outhouse and many others were built over these crevices to eliminate cleaning.

Photo and information courtesy Richard Vincent.

A Four-Story Outhouse and President Grant from Galena, Illinois

The DeSoto House, with more than 200 rooms for guests, was officially opened on April 9, 1855, and claimed to be the best hotel west of New York. It was named after Hernando DeSoto, the Spanish explorer who discovered the Mississippi River. It stood four stories on Main Street and five stories on Commerce Street. There was a court in the center of the building that was used for ventilation. A four-story outhouse was located in this court. Unfortunately, this classic privy was torn out during remodeling in 1960.

Abraham Lincoln spoke from the balcony of the DeSoto on July 23, 1856. His arch rival Stephen A. Douglas spoke from the same balcony two years later. (Douglas had courted Mary Todd Lincoln prior to her marriage to Abraham Lincoln.) U. S. Grant kept an office on the hotel's second floor during his eight years of presidency. Residents of Galena proudly explain that nine generals of the Civil War, including President Grant, came from Galena. The Galena Museum includes a large and beautiful Nast painting of Lee surrendering to General Grant.

The town was earlier known as La Pointe and Fever River. The name was changed to Galena in 1826, and the first post office in northern Illinois was established there the same year. Galena is the Latin name for lead sulphide, the chief ore of lead. By 1840, Galena was the wealthiest city in Illinois. Many of the first miners in Galena's lead mines were from Kentucky and Missouri. These miners suffered from the cold Illinois winters. They came up the river in keel boats in the spring and returned downstream in the fall. Their habits resembled those of the sucker fish that migrated seasonally up and down the Mississippi. It was in this manner that Illinois became known as the "Sucker State."

Information courtesy Richard Vincent.

CHAPTER 5
PRESIDENTIAL THRONES

Even big people used little houses. That included the presidents of our nation. Some of the wealthier people had brick outhouses. It was not until 1920 that presidents were elected by receiving votes of more than 10 percent of the free population. Jackson was elected by 5.8 percent in 1832. Lincoln was elected by 6.8 percent in 1860, Cleveland by 8.8 percent in 1884, Teddy Roosevelt by 9.5 percent in 1904, and Wilson by 8.9 percent in 1916.

Abraham Lincoln's Outhouse in Illinois

Abraham Lincoln must have believed in recycling, for his outhouse was not built with the usual bench-type seats. Instead, it was equipped with halves of three whiskey kegs. The seats were hand carved. This design was more desirable for accommodating ladies who wore the hoop skirts fashionable during the period. The Lincoln home in Springfield is one of the most significant associated with America's beloved sixteenth president. It is the only home Abraham Lincoln ever owned. He and Mrs. Lincoln lived in the home seventeen years. Lincoln walked twelve miles to school to get an education; no school bus, no hot lunches. (What a lousy PTA!)

Photo by Steven Johnson.

President George Washington Used It

That's what the sign said by this three holer. You will see numerous signs in eastern states that state "Washington slept here," but this is the only one I saw with this claim. Some of these early privies were built to last. A brick outhouse has often been a standard subject of American conversation. Very few are in actual use today. Bricks came into popular use as income increased. We do not know who built this outhouse or when, but it certainly was an elegant one in its day. The sign indicates that George Washington dropped some of his cares in this sturdy structure that has withstood the test of time.

Photo by Walter Weber.

President Jefferson's Outhouse in Virginia, the Panhandle State (10th State, 1788)

This 1940 picture of the entire south terrace at Monticello shows one of Jefferson's privies. There are five privies in the structure of Monticello: three in the house (in Jefferson's bedroom and the first- and second-floor south passages) and two attached to the L-shaped dependency wings. The house privies are vertical shafts from the cellar level to skylights at the roof level. A 160-foot-long brick tunnel leads from the base of these privies to a point southeast of the house. This "air tunnel" was presumably intended to ventilate the interior privies.

The external privies, or "necessaries" as Jefferson called them, are square stone buildings with stepped pyramidal roofs. Archaeological excavations near the north privy have uncovered another brick-lined tunnel, about twenty feet long. Findings so far suggest that this tunnel was a drain, possibly activated by flushing water from a cistern near the privy. The south privy has not yet been excavated.

Nothing is known about the workings of the interior privies. It has been suggested that a pot in each privy was raised and lowered by means of a pulley system. Nor is the method of removing the waste entirely clear. There is a door into one of the shafts in the cellar, but openings between each shaft are at a lower level. Note that Jefferson paid one of his slaves on a regular basis for cleaning the "sewers."

Photo and information courtesy Lucia C. Stanton, Director of Research, The Thomas Jefferson Memorial Foundation, Inc.

President Jackson's Necessary in Tennessee

This symbol of sturdiness and permanence belonged to our seventh president. It is located at the Hermitage near Nashville, and historians have concluded that it was built shortly after 1831. When first constructed, it had a simple square opening at the back for shoveling out accumulated waste.

In 1835, President Jackson became the first president to be subject to an assassination attempt. Because of his strength and energy, Jackson won the name of Old Hickory during the War of 1812.

Photo courtesy Ladies Hermitage Association.

President Hoover's Outhouse in Oregon, the Beaver State (33rd State, 1889)

Our thirty-first president was born in West Branch, Iowa, in 1874. Orphaned at nine, he then lived with an uncle, Dr. Minthorne, in Newburg, Oregon. Hoover was a successful mining engineer and the first man to rise to the presidency through business. Unfortunately, the Great Depression of the early thirties occurred during his presidency. You can see his cradle in the small home in which he was born. This old outhouse, with its warped and cracked boards, stands on the grounds of the Minthorne house in Newburg, Oregon. It has survived bottle collectors, old board collectors, and vandals. President Hoover also signed an act in 1931 making "The Star Spangled Banner" our national anthem.

Photo courtesy Lambert Florin, author of Backyard Classics.

President Johnson's Outhouse in Texas, the Lone Star State (28th State, 1845)

This was at LBJ's boyhood home in Johnson City, Texas. You are seeing three outhouses. Professor J. B. Outhouse and his granddaughter Karma are shown. "Outhouses have always been an essential part of the North American scene. The family name of Outhouse does not originate from the source. The name originated from the Dutch town Uithuizen which stood on a polder, reclaimed from the sea. As the people moved out to the polder, they were referred to as outerhouses. The name assumed the English spelling of outhouse in 1695. The one advantage in that people always remember our name."

Photo courtesy J. B. Outhouse, Professor Emeritus, Animal Science, Purdue University.

At the Herbert Hoover Birthplace in Iowa, the Hawkeye State (29th State, 1846)

Your eyes may deceive you, for this looks just like an outhouse. It is not an outhouse, but was built as a replica and is used for storage of tools. The Hoover library and museum is a very interesting place where you can see the first television.

Photo by Steven Johnson.

CHAPTER 6
HISTORICAL OUTHOUSES

Do you collect or like to see or hear about some particular type of antique? Do you belong to a group that talks about historical events or subjects? It is a popular thing to do these days. This chapter includes pictures of outhouses preserved by organizations or individuals interested in saving a slice of American history. In many cases, only the photographs have been preserved. A few pictures are of more recent vintage. Remember, today is tomorrow's history.

A Super Six Seater in Colorado

Yes, this really is an outhouse in Georgetown, Colorado. Georgetown was founded in 1859. In many cases, the outhouse was held in the same esteem as the residence it served; it was constructed of the same high quality materials and mirrored the architecture of the main building. When wealthy silver magnate W. A. Hammill struck it rich, he built this elaborate outhouse of the same architectural design as his mansion. The door you see at my right was the servants' entrance to three uniform pine seats. (See Chapter 9.) The family entrance on the side closest to the mansion had three walnut seats of variable size. Outhouses seldom have a porch. Maybe it was for those who could not or would not go away. The fancy outhouses, with gable roofs and fancy cupolas, were originally associated with more elaborate homes, but whether fancy or shabby, the aroma was about the same, day or night. This home has been turned into an interesting museum and preserved as the Hammill House.

Photo by Steven Johnson.

Pillar of the Past in South Carolina, the Palmetto State (8th State, 1788)

This outhouse can be seen at the South Carolina State Museum in Columbia. It was no longer needed in Spartanburg County after the Tabernacle Methodist Church added indoor plumbing. Tabernacle Methodist is best known as the church where Benjamin Wofford, founder of Spartanburg's Wofford College, worshipped. Rodger Stroup, curator of history for the South Carolina State Museum, said the outhouse was one of the most unusual artifacts they had collected. He explained that outhouses were becoming extinct and museum officials wanted to collect one while it was still available. Several museum employees are shown preparing it for moving.

Photo courtesy South Carolina State Museum.

A Centenarian in Delaware, the Blue Hen State (1st State, 1787)

Graced by a white porcelain doorknob, this privy door is similar to those used on doors in the early homes. This outhouse was built in 1885. Originally located on a farm just south of Clayton, Delaware, it is now part of the interesting Delaware Agricultural Museum, Dover. A few outhouses could tell you which way the wind was blowing. Most of the people kept theirs scrubbed, and the holes usually had a lid or board to keep them closed.

Photo courtesy the Delaware Agricultural Museum.

Distinctive in North Carolina

The hexagonal shape and the high roof of this old dooley are indications of special effort and pride. The picture was taken in 1955 in Hillsboro, North Carolina. Some of the shingles have surrendered to the elements, but the building remains mainly intact. In 1870, North Carolina became the first state to impeach a governor.

Photo courtesy the North Carolina Division of Archives and History.

A Historical Landmark in Texas

This deluxe three holer in Henderson is the first outhouse in Texas to be recognized by the Texas Historical Commission as a historically significant landmark. The official marker identifies the 1908 Arnold outhouse as being preserved to illustrate part of the lifestyle of nineteenth and early twentieth century Texas. It is larger than most standard outhouses, and the milled pattern on the front door and window facings matched that of the large house. The bench is equipped with large, medium, and small holes. Each has a lid with the original ironstone (ceramic) knob still in place. It has louvered windows on each side and, in the back, a pressed glass window measuring five inches by twenty-four inches. Much credit goes to Virginia Knapp, who heads the Rusk County Historical Society.

Photo courtesy the Texas Historical Commission.

Peaceful in Georgia, the Empire State of the South
(4th State, 1788)

"Don't sit under the apple tree with anyone else but me." Even if it wasn't an apple tree, this facility was useful in relieving a situation. Many privies were placed in a shady area. This four seater was built in Dooley County, Georgia, in 1889, before the days of nylon and dacron. It's a backyard jewel that has survived much wind and weather. It now sits under a pear tree at Georgia's Progressive Farmstead in Tipton. Georgia is also known as the Goober State.

Photo courtesy Georgia Agrirama, State Museum of Agriculture.

South Pass Discovered in Wyoming

It was 1830 when South Pass, Wyoming, was first used as a passageway for the first wagon trains crossing the Rocky Mountains. When the first gold was discovered in 1842, mining camps were resented by Native Americans because the miners killed the game and fouled the streams with sluicing. This log outhouse in South Pass City was built before sawed lumber was available. It is an example of where escape could be cut off, so it had portholes through which a rifle could be fired.

Photo courtesy Lambert Florin, author of Backyard Classics.

Two Ventilators in Wyoming

South Pass City, Wyoming, was a gateway for many of the westbound wagon trains, a stopping place for the Pony Express, and also the home of suffragette Esther Hobart Morris who obtained a full voting franchise for women in Wyoming. The large heart-shaped ventilator must have been an auxiliary. Other artistically carved symbols included crescents, quarter moons, stars, diamonds, and O's. The moon is said to represent the ladies while the star indicated men. These symbols were especially important during colonial times since only a small percentage of the people were able to write or read. The symbols were cut either in the door or side to allow light and ventilation. Many outhouses had no windows or ventilating ducts, and ventilation was a must.

Photo courtesy Lambert Florin, author of Backyard Classics.

We Never Close in Wyoming

Take your choice. The doors are unlabeled. In fact, one door is pushed over and the other is pushed in. The sagging doors are

an indication of old age in this monument of environmental protection. This old outhouse and the dilapidated old railroad station are about the only evidence that the town of Fossil ever existed. It is close to the Fossil National Monument west of Kemmerer. J. C. Penney opened his first store in Kemmerer, and his home there is now a historical site. This picture was taken in August 1988.

Photo by Walter Weber.

Twin Outhouses, One Wood Shed, in Illinois

This woodshed with a three seater on each side belonged to Supreme Court Justice David Davis, the man who encouraged Abraham Lincoln's nomination for the presidency. This cruciform building was designed by architect Alfred Piquenard, using details derived from the Italian villa style. It shares construction material with the adjacent mansion, including cream city brick, slate roofing, matching millwork, and paint scheme. The twin privies had finished interiors, painted window and door trim, whitewashed plaster walls and ceilings, and a wooden floor with baseboards. Wooden ducts exhausted the brick-lined pits below. (More details in Chapter 8.) These outhouses were for the servants.

Information courtesy Rebecca Landau; photo by Walter Weber.

Crowned in Connecticut, the Land of Steady Habits (5th State, 1788)

This 1788 privy—with its crowning ornament of a decorative knob—belonged to John Watson (1724-1824) of East Windsor Hill, Connecticut. The Watson home is the earliest three-story mansion still standing in the Connecticut Valley today. It is an early example of what would become the dominant building type for the elite in the period between 1783 and 1805. Both the mansion and outhouse were designed by famous architect Thomas Hayden (1745-1817), with the privy in the same style as the mansion. This was a pretty fancy privy. Strategically placed shrubs or a lattice wall were often used for privacy. Connecticut is also known as the Constitution State. In 1842, it became the first state to establish a public education system.

Photo courtesy the Connecticut Trust for Historic Preservation.

A Five Holer with a Fireplace in Virginia

Could this five holer have been the original site of a fireside chat? This mid-eighteenth century privy belonged to William Byrd of Westover, Charles County, Virginia. The extraordinary seating arrangement parallels—in a most private realm—the hierarchical system of contemporary Virginia courtrooms. Entering the building from a remarkably high set of steps, one passes between two rows of seats. Those to the left flank a fireplace, and they are small and low, presumably for the children. On the opposite wall, a brick apse has been constructed inside the square walls, forming the background for a semicircular seat that faces the fireplace. The seat is pierced by three holes. Those at the sides are of medium size, while that at the center is slightly

larger—for the expansive patriarch. This historically famous five seater from the 1700s has been preserved to show one phase of colonial life.

Photo and information courtesy Edward Chappel, Director of Architectural Research, Colonial Williamsburg; Neg. No. 83-4601S.

A Room for Two with a View in Massachusetts, the Bay State (6th State, 1788)

This nifty biffy in South Roynton, Massachusetts, belonged to Nathan Dean. It was built in the 1700s. The fancy roof is indicative of a fancy house, and this outhouse is evidence of the pride of those in the big house. The outhouse becomes an important shelter from stormy skies and offers respite from pain. This picture was taken in the course of the Historic American Buildings Survey in the 1930s and early 1940s. Basketball was invented in Massachusetts in 1891.

Photo by Arthur Haskell, courtesy the Society for the Preservation of New England Antiquities; Neg. No. 7915-AH.

The Judge's Rest House in Massachusetts

Only wealthy people could afford two privies. This double-entry eighteenth century privy belonged to Judge Holten in Danvers. With its paneled doors, large glass windows, and fancy roof, it was considered an elegant outhouse during pioneer days. Some people believed an outhouse was the most important building on the premises. Archaeologists have learned a great deal about eighteenth century American life by excavating privies. There were no sanitation trucks to gather trash and garbage. It was customary and convenient to use the privy for a place to throw old shoes, eyeglasses, cooking pots, bottles, printer's type, and other discards.

Photo by Arthur Haskell, courtesy the Society for the Preservation of New England Antiquities; Neg. No. 5821-AH.

A Cedar Tree Outhouse in Washington, the Evergreen State (42nd State, 1889)

It was a cedar tree that had its start before the beginning of the Revolutionary War. When big cedars reach a certain age, their interiors begin to die. Dry rot sets in and sort of hollows them out. The door is gone, but the bottom hinge is still there. This old cedar tree outhouse is located at the entrance to Bartheusen Park and is being preserved as a unique relic of our heritage. Hans Bartheusen came to Washington from Norway in 1883. He and his wife Lida set up housekeeping and stayed there all of their lives, so one presumes the stump privy was made at that time. The stump outhouse, an old barn full of relics, and the park were donated to the city of Lynden at the time of Bartheusen's death in 1944.

Photo courtesy Fred Parks and Tom Murray.

An Outhouse Out Back at the Jesse James Home

This Victorian-style, two-holer, plastered outhouse matched the house it originally served in Edgerton, Missouri. Its new resting place is the back yard of the Jesse James Home in St.

Joseph, Missouri (the house where Jesse was killed). Mrs. Vivion Nash of Edgerton donated the unflushable. Built before the turn of the century, it is a real jewel. Not many are found with a gable roof.

Photo and information courtesy the Patee House Museum.

Pioneer Privy in South Dakota, the Coyote State (44th State, 1889)

Dovetailed log cabins and their accompanying log outhouses were built from 1640 to 1860. Many early churches were also built of logs. This real pioneer log outhouse has defied years of the elements. Spaces between the logs were sealed with clay and grass to keep out snow, rain, and cold. This one is north of Swift Bird Cemetery along the highway near Cheyenne Agency, Dewey County. Extremely cold weather often caused the build-up of outhouse stalagmites under the seats. In some cold areas, it was a common practice to take along a lighted kerosene lantern to create heat—and its resulting comfort—even during daytime visits.

Photo courtesy the South Dakota State Historical Society and State Agricultural Heritage Museum.

Sodhouse in Nebraska, the Cornhusker State (37th State, 1867)

This 1887 sodhouse of the Bergert family was built near Westerville, Nebraska. The family also had a supplemental little house out back. A sodhouse was said to be warm in winter and cool in summer. In some areas, a sodhouse was the first home for many pioneers. Sodhouse construction was explained to me in 1933, the first year I taught at Remington, Indiana. An eighty-five-year-old man showed me the raised areas in his lawn that outlined the sodhouse in which he was born. He explained how

the builder needed a team of horses, a plow, and a square-pointed shovel. The sod was cut into lengths about two feet long and six inches thick. These were laid up like concrete blocks. A ridgepole was set across the top of the gable ends with a strong pole in the center for support. Smaller poles were then laid over the ridgepole, after which sod and dirt were spread across the new roof. The durable, large, and heavy grindstone was used to sharpen axes, scythes, butcher knives, and other tools.

*Photo courtesy the
Solomon D. Butcher Collection,
Nebraska State Historical Society.*

Sharing the Shade in North Carolina, the Tarheel State (12th State, 1788)

This unpretentious outhouse and tree seem to have shared the same spot for many years. The large, louvered ventilator probably provided plenty of fresh air. Early pioneers had to devote much time to themselves and the effects of an antagonistic environment, but there was one universal problem that confronted every citizen and visitor in every state of the nation: where to go. In some cases, people were advised to bang on the outhouse door before entering, in order to arouse the snakes lying on the ledges. People also involuntarily entertained bats, bees, flies, hornets, lizards, mice, porcupines, rats, scorpions, spiders, and wasps.

Photo courtesy the North Carolina Division of Archives and History..

Preservation Privy in Indiana

This truly unique Switzerland County privy is a national landmark located near the county courthouse in Vevay, Indiana. An elegant structure for everybody's relief. It is listed and described in the Historic American Building Survey for Indiana. The brick, one-story, hexagonal outhouse has a small louvered cupola in the center and a standing-seam metal roof. It was probably built in 1864. The photo was taken in 1971.

Photo courtesy the Historic Landmarks Foundation of Indiana

Services Were Short Here in Minnesota

This well-preserved two-hole outhouse is located back of the Frontenac Episcopal Church and is still functional. The church structure was built through the efforts of General Nathaniel Collins McLean who took up residence in Frontenac after the Civil War. It is not known if this was the original outhouse, but

none of the older church members recall a different one. The outhouse formerly had a wooden door handle, now replaced by a metal latch. Many outhouses were covered with grape vines, wisteria, trumpet vine, or morning glories.

Information courtesy John R. Hodgins, M.D.; photo courtesy the Minnesota Historical Society.

Four in Florida, the Peninsula State (27th State, 1845)

These four of a kind almost looked alike, but the fourth one has a different entrance. If you want to guess, one could be for the wife, one for the husband, one for the children, and one for guests—or family, neighbors, strangers.

Photo courtesy Florida Photographic Collection, Florida State Archives.

Whitewashed in Maryland, the Old Line State (7th State, 1788)

This little whitewashed outhouse in Westminister, Maryland, probably played an important role in providing satisfaction and relief a century ago. This picture was part of a composite photo taken in Westminister in 1888. The outhouse was in the view that looked back over the city from the campus, located on the northwestern outskirts of town. Western Maryland College was founded as a private academy in 1860. It was reorganized as a college under the supervision of the Methodist church in 1886. There were no frills on this outhouse. This was definitely in the days before clothes dryers.

Photo courtesy the Maryland State Archives; G 1477-6362.

A Lonely Leaner in Florida

This relic is on its last lean in Florida. It will never be as well-known as the Leaning Tower of Pisa. An outhouse will be remembered as a place where a man never feels obligated to give up his seat to a lady. Apparently, the door is reclining on the ground.

Photo courtesy Florida Photographic Collection, Florida State Archives.

Lonely in New Mexico, the Sunshine State (47th State, 1912)

This weather-battered privy seems to be standing all alone and erect, like a sentinel dejected and forlorn. It looks deserted, but maybe it was designed for pleasant use in one's spare time.

Outhouses served as hospitality houses for people of all ages. Many outdoor inconveniences have succumbed to the ravages of time and collectors of old bottles. This 1954 picture is from Acoma Pueblo.

Photo by Henry D. Tefft, courtesy the Museum of New Mexico; Neg. No. 106178

Dutch Doors in Montana

Some privies were hastily constructed with rough lumber. This old outhouse with Dutch doors was different enough to be distinctive. It was found at an abandoned homestead up Bruce Creek near Montana City. Built for utility, not for beauty, it was probably like a bank, accepting big or small deposits.

Photo by Peter Meloy, courtesy the Montana Historical Society.

Eureka in Nevada

Eureka is a term used when discovering a triumph. Silver was first discovered in Eureka, Nevada, in 1864. It is probably one of the best preserved mining towns in Nevada. Ronald M. James, Deputy State Historic Preservation Officer, kindly advised me about the location of this four seater with its ornate Italianate gables: it stood close to Route 50. Susan Gallaghu, Eureka County Historical

Society, provided the details of its construction in the 1920s by Frank Bartine, owner of Eureka Cabins. Typical of early Twenties motor lodge architecture, the Cabins are now known as the Eureka Motel. Bartine later moved the outhouse to his ranch about thirty miles west. President Reagan attended Eureka College in Eureka, Illinois.

Photo and information courtesy Susan Gallaghu, Eureka County Historical Society.

Almost an Inhouse in Idaho

Bonanza, Idaho, is an old ghost town. Large silver mining camps were located in the Bonanza area. Winters were cold, snow was deep, but this outhouse was almost built into the log cabin, providing instant all-season service. This built-in outhouse was so convenient that snowshoes were not needed.

Photo courtesy Lambert Florin, author of Backyard Classics.

High and Mighty in Idaho

A mighty handy steep drop. You didn't need high boots, and it was a cinch to shovel off the snow when you had to go. This handy house in Silver City had plenty of deposit space, and you didn't need to worry about a clean-out. The heavy rains in the spring would raise Jordan Creek high enough to wash

HISTORICAL OUTHOUSES

away all accumulation. Construction of most early privies was according to the carpenter's idea. (He carried the plan in his head.)

Photo copyright 1988 by Norman D. Weis, from The Two Story Outhouse, Caxton Printers Ltd. See Appendix.

Handy to the House in Louisiana

This is about as close as one could locate the privy and still go out back. The vise and crosscut saw (left) indicate the owner kept his tools real handy. The hame (right) is evidence that he used horses or mules. Apparently, the builder was oblivious of any danger from a close-in outhouse.

Photo courtesy the Louisiana State Museum.

An Octogenarian in Illinois

This old 1900 outhouse has weathered more than eighty years of cold winters and hot summers near Milford, Illinois. With a window on each side, the occupant had an adequate source of light to read most any kind of catalog or whatever was available. A few shingles are gone and the path has grown over, but it is still there in an emergency.

Photo courtesy Bill Kerchanfaught.

An Eight Sider in Pennsylvania, the Keystone State (2nd State, 1787)

This beautiful, well-kept, pre-plumber, rugged old outhouse is one of the sturdiest. It is located on the Curtiss Valley estate about five miles from Waymart, Pennsylvania. This very rare, eight-sided, small-scale edifice dates back to 1830.

Photo and information courtesy Larry Schott, Waymire, Pennsylvania.

A Shady Asset in West Virginia, the Mountain State
(35th State, 1863)

Most outhouses were built in the backyard. This early American institution is greatly neglected and often forgotten. This one rests in the shade at Mussellville, Fayette County, West Virginia. (P.S. The dog is also resting in the shade.)

*Photo by Greg Clark, courtesy
the West Virginia Department of Culture and History.*

CHAPTER 7
RELAXICATING RENDEZVOUSES– RESERVATIONS REQUESTED

There was a wide variety of styles. Many were quaint, matchless, far-reaching.

Take It with You in Montana

The Cooper brothers built this "home groan" camper complete with a back porch and a tag-along portable privy. The Cooper brothers are widely known for their excellent travelogues spiced with lots of clean humor. An outhouse was a mighty welcome sight to weary travelers.

Photo courtesy Dennis and Betty Cooper.

Before Trick or Treat in Utah, the Beehive State
(45th State, 1896)

It was considered fun and traditional to upset someone's outhouse on Halloween. The privy (this one is from Manti, Utah) was a prime target when youngsters could tip it over. There was no age limit to those pranksters. (Some were old enough to vote.) Groups of boys moved swiftly and silently. Outhouses were occasionally moved to roofs of buildings. The big, massive, well-anchored ones could not be pushed over. Harold Barkhau of Indianapolis told me about the time he and some other boys turned over the outhouse belonging to a Gus Seyford who lived on Pleasant Run Boulevard. They waited until they saw him go into the outhouse, but they didn't wait to see how he got out of it. Just tricks, no treats.

Photo courtesy the Utah State Historical Society.

For the Fresh-Air Enthusiast in Utah

Cool all season. This air-conditioned two holer from Spring City, Utah, is fully automatic: no thermostats, no electric bills, no windows to break, no porch to fix, no locks to lock, and you never have to fumble for the key. The throne-like seating arrangement keeps one in high spirits. It doesn't really provide great gobs of privacy, but everyone has to go sometimes. Some of the outhouses were not in a superb condition of repair, so it sometimes took a certain amount of courage to sit down, especially on a frosty piece of timber.

Photo courtesy the Utah State Historical Society.

Air Conditioning and Tranquility in Michigan

Tranquility of mind, bathed in sunlight, plenty of exhilaration, and the maximum of solar energy. This fresh-air privy near Hannahville in Menominee County looks like a tornado has gone through, or did some people run short of firewood? Nice and cool in hot weather, this unique construction allows for ample cross ventilation. It also readily admits huge volumes of top quality natural light. Open 24 hours. It's for go, not for show.

Photo courtesy State Archives of Michigan.

Frozen Assets in Michigan

Snow, snow, beautiful, abominable snow! Outhouses and snow drifts have a common feature—freezing. The first activity after a heavy snowfall was to shovel a path to the privy. On some cold, wintry days, it seemed like pure power and endurance were not sufficient in themselves to bring about success. The trip was often unrelentingly tenuous. It took a mighty bold person with a great amount of courage to venture out there on wintry days. To say it was tough is putting it mildly. Visitors didn't tarry very long. Any person who never used one can't imagine how cold that seat was. This picture brings chilling memories of excursions to the privy. Was this the justification for red flannels? One of the reasons for having covers over the holes in wintertime was to help retain some of the warmth in the body waste and prevent the buildup of stalagmites. This picture is in a collection of photos from the Michigan State Police.

Photo courtesy State Archives of Michigan.

Balance of Nature in Mississippi, the Magnolia State
(20th State, 1817)

The true law of nature is progress and development; nature knows no pause. Self-preservation is the first law of man, and in this case, it was the law of the outhouse. In some cases, the man would provide partial privacy by building a partition about

halfway up so the people could carry on a conversation while taking care of their needs. Does Darwin's law of the survival of the fittest apply here? Some old outhouses never die, they just smell that way.

Photo courtesy of a friend.

Braced against All Worries

This privy leans to the belief that self-preservation is the first law of outhouses as well as man. Getting to this biffie was probably a task for the sure-footed or for those with only one thing in mind. It is not advisable to borrow the supporting pole.

Photo courtesy Lambert Florin, author of Backyard Classics.

Fatigued and Exhausted in Wyoming

What if a person suddenly gets a stomach ache? This one looks like it is near the final portion of an illustrious career. This tired old outhouse in South Pass City, Wyoming, seems to have served its time and is on its last lean. Its spirits are sagging, and it is about to collapse from weariness. This sagging structure has graciously aged through the years and is giving the impression of pride for having served well and belonging to another era. A herd of Hereford cattle was leisurely grazing in the same pasture. My wife kept an eye on that huge bull; fortunately, he was more contented eating grass than investigating my camera. The State of Wyoming is preserving and restoring what is left of South Pass City. It was still mostly a ghost town when we took this picture.

Photo by Walter Weber.

Plumbingless Privies in New Mexico

These are only a few of many privies seen on a high plateau in an old Indian pueblo– Acoma, "City in the Sky," one of Cortes's Seven Cities of Cibola. These private, single-purpose structures are perched on bare limestone rock near the pueblo's outskirts. In many cases, lime was used in outhouses, not for whitewash, but as an odor depressant. It was customary to keep a bucket or sack of lime in the outhouse to conceal any unpleasant aroma. A small scoop was often an accessory for transferring the lime into the hole. In some cases, people used wood ashes.

Photo courtesy National Animal Damage Control Association.

For Go, Not for Show, in New Mexico

Was this a futuristic model or a "do-it-yourself?" This specialized masterpiece is from Riley, an early Spanish farming, ranching, and mining settlement. It looks like a Depression-era outhouse; at least there is no interior plumbing. One of the accepted names for an outhouse was "Chic Sale." It was in 1929 that Charles Sale wrote *The Specialist.* He wrote that one should always build the outhouse so that the woodpile is between it and the house, that way your wood box is always full. He also wrote, "Paint her red and trim her in white, and you will always have a mighty, mighty pretty privy."

Photo courtesy National Animal Damage Control Association.

Well Ventilated in New Mexico

Would you say this small-scale edifice is a winterized privy? This one is near Madrid, a coal town started in the 1890s and run by a railroad. It experienced a revival in the 1960s when new people moved in. Privacy is quite variable, ranging from hastily hung blankets to elaborate doors. Hazards lurked in some outhouses. One of the hazards associated with outhouses was the possibility of bites from the black widow spider and the brown

recluse spider. Both have been found in privies. The male black widow spider does not bite. The bite from the female produces a slight swelling and two red spots may occur. Deaths have been reported in the very young, the aged, and those with hypertension. The brown recluse spider has been responsible for a number of cases of neurotic spider poisoning, and several deaths have been reported. On occasion, men have been bitten on the scrotum and have died from the resulting infection. There have also been cases of rat bites.

Photo courtesy National Animal Damage Control Association.

CHAPTER 8
MAY I BE EXCUSED?

There was one universal question, "May I be excused?" This was a very familiar question with all teachers. Both boys and girls asked their teacher for permission to take time off for personal needs. At one time, this involved going to the little special building usually located in the corner of the schoolyard.

Segregation in Iowa

This pair of outhouses was located at a rural school in Jackson County, Iowa. The picture was taken in the early 1930s. Boys' and girls' facilities were discreetly placed at opposite ends of the schoolyard. It is quite plausible that part of the time spent in the outhouse was for the explicit purpose of hiding from the teacher. The picture is similar to the one-room school that I attended near Melvin, Illinois, during the 1920s. There was no electricity, so our illumination came from the window on the north side. There was a teacher's desk and a long recitation bench where each grade sat during their portion of recitation. A large coal-fired stove in the rear of the school kept some of the children warm. The ink froze during the night, there was no running water, and a three-gallon bucket of water had to be obtained each morning from the closest neighbor. Everybody drank out of the same long-handled dipper.

The daily activity started with recitation of the Lord's Prayer and the Pledge of Allegiance. The four R's included reading, writing, arithmetic, and recitation. Strict discipline was present in most schools. There was an old saying: "Reading, writing, and arithmetic, taught to the tune of a hickory stick." In my case, the hickory stick was a razor strap hanging on the wall behind the teacher's desk, probably for psychological effect. One day, two boys sneaked that razor strap out of the schoolhouse and deposited it in the depth of the boys' toilet. One of the boys was named Walter Weber.

Photo courtesy the State Historical Society of Iowa.

A Three Holer in Arkansas, the Wonder State
(25th State, 1836)

This three holer was thought to be associated with a Kingston, Arkansas, school. The photo was taken in 1981. Small rural schools were close to settlements in the early days. The country schools were community schools. The philosophy was that a community with a school was a community with a future. In some cases, a person would build a school just for his family. He also built a small one-door outhouse. In some areas, the schoolhouse would be moved to a more convenient or more densely populated area. Thousands of people migrated to America in the nineteenth and early twentieth centuries who could not speak or read English. The early pioneer teachers were not blessed with numerous books and teaching aids. How would you teach a person to associate a name with an object? Some of the teachers (not necessarily in Arkansas) used mail-order catalogs because they were so well illustrated. Those were the days before students used computers to solve mathematics problems, so they learned arithmetic. They did not have word processors to correct their spelling.

Photo courtesy the Shiloh Museum, Springdale, Arkansas.

A Heated Outhouse at School in Montana

The Corbin, Montana, school provided a heated outhouse, a hospitality house for all ages. This picture was taken by Peter Meloy in September 1970. Life was not easy for the teachers or the pupils in those early days. Let's look at the Montgomery Ward catalog. Montgomery Aaron Ward started his company in 1872. His tenth catalog in 1874 had four pages. His eleventh catalog was 3 inches by 5 $1/2$ inches with thirty-two pages. By 1876, it had 152 pages, size 7 inches by 9 $1/2$. By 1892, it had 568 pages, with 8,000 illustrations. The 1911 issue had seventy-two illustrations on page 140 (Chapter 10 includes several). Thousands of copies were mailed out twice a year. The company discontinued its mail-order business in 1986.

Photo by Peter Meloy, courtesy the Montana Historical Society.

A Schoolhouse Outhouse in Nebraska

This outhouse, with its two entrances, was part of the public school grounds in Ogallala, Nebraska. One readily available supplementary teaching aid (not necessarily in Nebraska) was the Sears Roebuck catalog. Since it was so well illustrated, it was

often used to help immigrants learn the names of familiar items. Richard Warren Sears started selling watches in 1886. Al Roebuck repaired watches and joined Sears in 1887. They incorporated in 1893. Roebuck resigned shortly after that. Sears must have been a good psychologist; his catalog mirrored the needs and dreams of its readers. He editorialized and informed by illustrations. The 1893 catalog had 196 pages, the 1894 copy had 322 pages, and the 1895 catalog had 507 pages. By 1902, it had grown to 1,162 pages, 8 inches by 11 $^1/_2$. All of the pages were well illustrated; page 28, for example, featured 112 illustrations. The 1902 issue included a pull-chain water closet described as a "hopper closet." By 1905, the company was printing two million copies of its catalog. The 1902 Sears catalog has been partially reproduced, and it is said to be the second fastest selling book, with the Holy Bible number one.

Photo courtesy the Nebraska State Historical Society.

Privy Privileges in Nebraska

This one-room school was eight miles northwest of York, Nebraska. Reverend W. J. Gans, a Lutheran minister, taught the twenty-three students. Reverend Gans is buried at Middle Creek Lutheran Church eight miles east of Seward, Nebraska. This picture was taken about 1890 and was donated to the Nebraska State Historical Society by Reverend Gans's son, Theodore G. Gans. Some of the early schools reflected the designs of churches. The records show that a severe blizzard occurred here in 1888; the children were kept in the school overnight and picked up by their parents the next day. You can see an outhouse in the background. Many children living on farms and ranches at-

tended one-room schools where the restroom consisted of an outhouse. In some cases, there was only one facility, so the girls used it first, then the boys had their turn, and then it was time for recess. On some occasions, the trips to the outhouse were accompanied by the watchful eye of the teacher. It has also been reported that in some cases the early schools did not have an outhouse. The girls went out in the shrubbery one way, and the boys went the other way. Sometimes, there were separate entrances to the schoolhouse for boys and girls.

Photo courtesy the Nebraska State Historical Society.

A Sod Schoolhouse in Nebraska

Before there was a little old red schoolhouse, there was this little old sod schoolhouse in Nebraska. A successful school needed at least one outhouse, preferably two. This picture of an abandoned sod schoolhouse was taken from a postcard mailed on November 9, 1909, when the postage was only one cent. The earliest sod schoolhouse had a dirt floor, and soft mud was used for mortar. The sod roof and walls were a haven for snakes, rodents, and other small animals. The primary cash outlay was

for windows, a cast-iron stove, and paint for the blackboard. The veteran outhouse stands in solitude.

Photo courtesy the Nebraska State Historical Society.

CHAPTER 9
PLEASE BE SEATED

The number of holes and their size usually depended on the size of the family or the location of the facility. In some cases, the carpenter didn't really give much consideration to comfort. Sometimes the benches were too high or too low. In certain situations, the holes were too far back or too close to the front. The holes were occasionally too large, so there was danger of the children becoming wedged or falling through. It was inconvenient for adults when the hole was too small. In many cases, the carpenter carried the plans in his head.

Four in a Row, But Where to Go?

What happened to it? Did it fall victim to vandals, wind, or old age? There was no trace of a hotel, school, or hospital, but you can see it wasn't just for three at a time. The story is told that an outhouse of similar capacity was built at a red-light house, but the madame in charge had it torn down and replaced by four individual one holers. She explained that the girls spent too much time gossiping when "out there together." This old relic has survived for many years after the area was abandoned.

Photo and information courtesy Lambert Florin, author of Backyard Classics.

Three of a Kind in California

It was almost three of a kind in Bodie. At least the builder had an artistic touch and did a good job with his keyhole saw so that all of the holes are round. He customized the interior to most any posterior. Children have a priority on the middle seat. It's all in the family, but some privies had a standard level for grownups and a lower height for children. That is something you don't see in today's bathroom. Apparently, the lids on the big folks' seats would prevent a fall out or fall in. There is more to a privy than meets the nose. Bodie was a booming mining district after gold was discovered in 1860. At one time, it had about sixty-five saloons. The surviving buildings are under the supervision of the National Park Service.

Photo courtesy Lambert Florin, author of Backyard Classics.

Two Showing and One to Raise in Illinois

These three seats are in the Judge Davis outhouse in Bloomington, Illinois (see Chapter 6). This portion is not normally shown, but Rebecca Landau kindly unlocked the door so that this picture could be taken. The outhouse was finished in 1872. Archaeologists removed the floor in the summer of 1987 to determine the type of artifacts discarded in the pit. The brick-lined pit is 7 feet by 7 feet by 8 $^1/_2$ feet deep (I measured it). In some cases, archaeologists have found that the flat needles of hemlocks and yews were used prior to our current nice soft bathroom tissue. From the number of whiskey bottles found during excavations of old outhouses, it would appear that whiskey smell was masked by stronger smells.

Photo by David Weber.

Recycled in the Outhouse in New Mexico

This heart-shaped seat provided maximum comfort. This outhouse was built prior to the 1920s and is located near Colfax, New Mexico, a farming community. Many old Sears Roebuck and Montgomery Ward catalogs served a dual purpose: they

also provided interesting reading material while the occupant was sitting there, biding time. They became less valuable in reverse proportion to the increase in the quantity of slick pages.

Photo courtesy National Animal Damage Control Association.

Round or Square in California

This pair is from Bodie, California. Is that what is meant by being on the square? Perhaps the square hole with rough edges

discouraged visiting and hastened departure. One could relax beyond the urgency of the situation if the rounds or ovals were properly beveled, sanded, and smoothed.

Photo courtesy Lambert Florin, author of Backyard Classics.

A Comfortable Seat in Virginia

This is one of the seats in the previously shown five-seater brick outhouse from colonial days (see Chapter 6). The fireplace and comfortable seat offered maximum convenience. The rat hole near the floor (left side) is evidence that rats were also a problem in colonial days.

Photo courtesy Colonial Williamsburg; Neg. No. 83-4608S.

Chapter 10
Inhouse Outhouses

The whole idea in moving the outhouse indoors was comfort and convenience. The ideas and facilities varied as evidenced by the following pictures. The big transition period started in the 1920s when facilities were beginning to change from outdoors to indoors, from outhouses to inhouses.

The Ultimate Inhouse Outhouse in South Dakota

When Marquis De Mores built his twenty-six room chateau in South Dakota's badlands back in 1883, he wanted convenience for his lady named Medora. He placed the privy on the bottom floor so that the lady would not have to venture out into the cold winter weather. You can see it was complete with an appropriate ventilation duct.

Photo courtesy Bob Ross, author of Muddled Meanderings in an Outhouse.

— THE UNFLUSHABLES

An Outhouse In House in Neckerzimmer, Germany

You are looking at a strategically located turret on Germany's famous Hornberg Castle. This unit provides a convenient seating place for a person's posterior without having to leave the comforts of the castle. The discoloration on the walls provides evidence that the exterior addendum served the occupants' daily needs. Tours of the castle do not include use of this unique facility.

Hornberg Castle is located on the Neckar River, about an hour's drive south of Heidelberg. The visitor's brochure includes historic events dating back to about 150 A.D. Bishop Henry of Speyer bought the castle and the villages of Zimmern, Steinbeck, and Stockbronn in 1259. The castle was the eastern fortress of the Diocese Speyer. Bishop Mathias sold the castle to Lutz Schott of Schottenstein in 1467, and he sold it with all attached properties to Knight Gotz von Berlihengen in 1517. Knight Gotz lost his right hand in the battle of Landshut in 1504, and so he had a hook on his right arm. He was a leader in the Farmers (Peasant) War in 1525. I took this picture with me while attending the annual meeting of the Indiana German Heritage Society, hoping that one of the members could provide more information. Fortunately, Clemens Huppe from Pffenweller, Germany, was a visitor. He told me that a similar arrangement could be seen at the Hochkonigsburg Castle in Breisach, France.

Photo by Pat Hilliard, courtesy Kenneth Johnson.

A Built-In Privy in Illinois

This privy is an integral part of the Galena blacksmith shop, where it is built right into the wall. An approximately one-foot opening near the bottom provides access for cleaning. There was no outside entrance.

Photo and information courtesy Richard Vincent and Alfred Mueller.

Inside No Holer in Illinois

One size fits everybody. The seat in this no holer in the Galena blacksmith shop consists of a long two-by-four which has been smoothed off on top. The area from the two-by-four to the floor is enclosed. A person could stand up to it or hang his posterior over it, whichever meets the requirement. This was similar to some of the other early privies which did not have any holes but only a

heavy timber or rail inside from wall to wall serving as a seat and support. These were uncomfortable and dangerous. This type accommodates all sizes and all shapes in any season. Just one bit of caution: One should not lean back.

Photo courtesy Richard Vincent.

Some Outhouses Were Not Out, In Illinois

Before the availability of indoor plumbing, some privies were built inside of other structures as part of the garage, woodshed, cob house, utility building, or back porch. A door opening inward enabled a person to sit in peace and quiet while enjoying lots of fresh air and, in some cases, sunlight or moonlight. The door could be closed quickly in case of approaching footsteps and held shut with the foot. This inside outhouse (and many others) included a ventilating duct to carry the foul air from under the seat to the area above the ceiling. This inside privy was different from the average outhouse built over a pit. It was equipped with a large removable drawer that slid on the ground under the seats. A large iron ring on one end enabled the owner to have it pulled out and then dragged away after which the contents were disposed of in a suitable manner. It was then sanitized and reinstated for further usage.

Photo by Walter Weber.

Mrs. Lincoln's Chamber Pot in Illinois

Prior to the advent of the flush toilet, the traditional modes of indoor waste disposal were based on the use of the chamber pot or "slop jar" indoors. Located in each bedroom, the chamber pots were usually made of fine porcelain and generally decorated with delicate patterns. Some folks even had specially decorated household vessels for company. The slop jar was commonly a bucket with a handle and contoured top and a lid. It was emptied the next morning, thoroughly washed, and usually allowed to dry in the sun. This one was shown in Mrs. Abraham Lincoln's bedroom in Springfield, Illinois. The household vessels used by royalty were frequently made of gold, silver, onyx, or brass. Less expensive portable potties were made of enameled iron.

Photo by Walter Weber.

Montgomery Ward's Indoor Waste Disposal Equipment

The 1897 Montgomery Ward catalog featured a sanitary commode for $2.50. The 1911 catalog listed an enamel combinet or slop jar for $1.37. An odorless commode was priced at 69 cents while an enameled iron chamber was available for 19 cents. Although most American homes had one or more portable potties prior to indoor plumbing, they were often reserved for sick room or emergency use during inclement weather. Several historians have reported that, prior to indoor plumbing in certain European cities, some of the unscrupulous people would empty their boudoir potties by hurling the contents out of the upstairs window. It has also been said that the custom of a man walking closest to the curb was to prevent his lady from stepping into that waste.

Pictures and information courtesy Emmett D. Chisum, American Heritage Center, University of Wyoming.

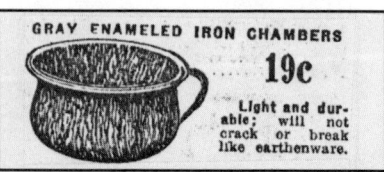

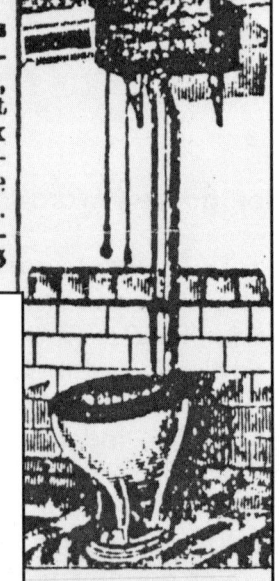

Mrs. Lincoln's Sanitary Commode, Illinois

You will see this one in Abraham Lincoln's Springfield home. The sanitary commode could be used in any room or moved to the side of the bed for the sick. The receptacle for waste was usually enamel and readily removed.

Photo by Steven Johnson.

CHAPTER 11
LIGHTENING THE LOAD—
POSTED PRIVIES

Humor brings pleasant relief from painful experiences. Good clean humor aims for amusement, happiness, joy, and merriment, but not always laughter.

Enter at Your Own Risk in Ontario, Canada

Signs of the humorous at heart are sometimes reflected on the outhouse. If we risk a little humor, we can lift barriers, lighten our loads, rise above limitations, and keep going. People around the world enjoy clean humor. This sign was on an outhouse near Vermillion Bay, Ontario.

Photo by Walter Weber.

Complying With OSHA in Washington State

Many of our problems never existed until someone in Washington, D.C., appointed a committee to investigate. OSHA issued a regulation that field workers should have a facility within five minutes of walking distance. OSHA did not specify how fast the people should walk. Don Richardson from Pomoroy, Washing-

ton, expressed humor by attaching a trailer on his combine and constructing an outhouse which he identified as OSHA. It was even complete with a Sears Roebuck catalog. Did you ever visit one of those fields in certain areas of China or India? At least the American architecture of the past has a throne.

Photo courtesy Don Richardson.

It May be Habit Forming in Ontario, Canada

Humor is a great virtue, and in this case, it was a reminder to form the habit of using the outhouse on a regular basis. This sign was found nailed on the outhouse door at Big Canon Lake in Ontario. It did turn out to be a daily habit.

Photo by Walter Weber.

Ever See the Arctic Circle? In Northwest Territory, Canada

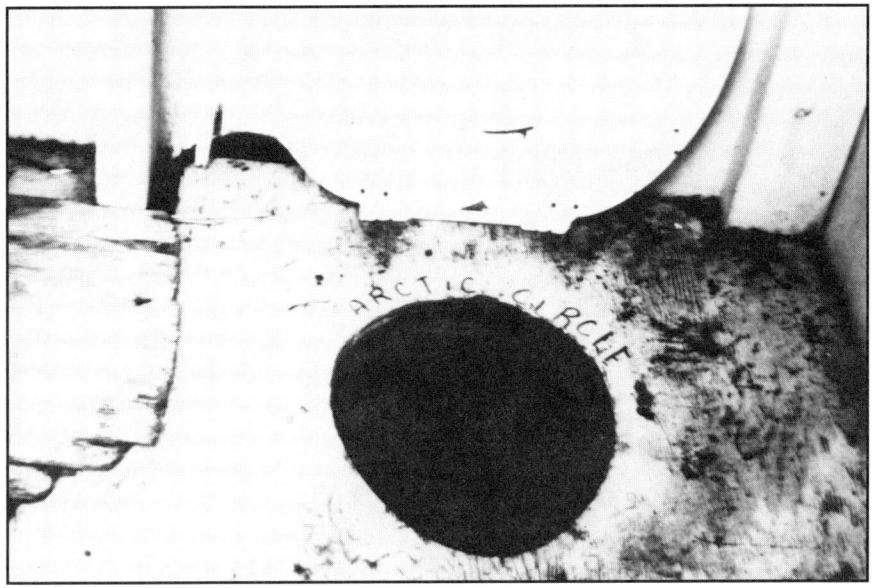

I didn't see the Arctic Circle in 1967 when my wife, son Steven, and I flew over it on our way to Point Barrow, the farthest north city in North America. If you watched the rescue efforts for the whales on your TV in the fall of 1988, you saw the picture of the Top of the World Hotel. We stayed in that hotel. Our room had two small single beds and one five-gallon bucket for sanitation purposes. We were told the five-gallon buckets were emptied into a fifty-gallon drum and then taken out to the tundra. I flew over the Arctic Circle again on a fishing trip to Great Bear Lake, about 1,500 miles north of Winnipeg, and still didn't see it. After spending all that money to reach Great Bear Lake, it was easy to decide to take advantage of a fly-out to try to catch Arctic char. I finally saw the Arctic Circle located inside the outhouse where some previous fisherman had thoughtfully identified it with his felt pen. An Arctic adventure. Now you have seen the Arctic Circle!

My friend Gerald Wunsch, who lived in Alaska in 1953, explained how the honey buckets were placed under the toilet seats and emptied daily into a fifty-five gallon oil drum. The drum was placed as far away from the home as possible. Those drums would freeze solid in the wintertime when they would be collected on a flatbed truck and hauled away. He was positive that they were not buried in the frozen tundra. His mother bought a Sears catalog chemical toilet which became the talk of the town.

Photo by Walter Weber.

One-Hour Parking in New Mexico

The sign says, "One Hour Parking, Police Department." Does that time limit refer to the vehicle or to use of the facility? The normal situation was no speed limit and no time limit. Many of the old weathered outhouses have served their purpose for more than half a century. This picture was taken in 1946.

Photo by Ferenz Fedor, courtesy the Museum of New Mexico; Neg. No. 102020.

Corncobs, Catalogs, and Containers in Illinois

The use of corncobs in the outhouse is not a tall tale. Many of the outhouses in the corn-growing states were equipped with a wooden box that held corncobs, old newspapers, and last year's mail-order catalogs. However, these cobs had been through the corn sheller and so were relatively smooth. The box was often a wooden box which had been used for shipping dried apricots or dried prunes. Prior to 1914, it was unlawful to ship food in anything except a wood or metal box. Corncobs were mentioned by James Whitcomb Riley in his poem (see Chapter 13). Corncobs were used as a fuel in cook stoves and for starting fires of coal or wood in fireplaces and heating stoves. One of the after-school chores for farm boys was to keep the cob basket replenished prior to supper time. Now corncobs have entered a new era. A recent article by *Indianapolis Star* correspondent Ernest A. Wilkinson explains that more than sixty new uses have been found for corncobs besides corncob pipes. In addition to being a good livestock feed, they are being used in corncob flour, industrial abrasives, imitation maple syrup, explosives, hand soap abrasives, pesticide carriers, cosmetics, feedstock for sugar, and pharmaceuticals.

Photo by Bill Kerchanfaut.

No Parking, 10 to 12 A.M., Wednesdays Only, in Brazil

People around the world enjoy a little clean humor. Somebody translocated this "No Parking" sign to this fresh-air outhouse in Brazil, South America. The facility probably serves both Senoras and Senoritas.

Photo courtesy Professor Fred Warren, Purdue University.

No Dumping in Colorado

Under penalty of law in Goldfield, Colorado. Goldfield is close to Victor, where Lowell Thomas grew up, and close to Cripple Creek, where gold was first discovered in 1891. Nearly 500 gold mines were operating in the area at the turn of the century. The Cripple Creek area was one of the most famous gold fields in the world. Who do you suppose nailed the "No Dumping" sign on this old outhouse?

Photo by Steven Johnson.

A Pair of Summer Houses

If someone talks about summer houses, your first reaction might be that they are for use during the summer. His answer would be: "No, sum-er-fur men, and sum-er-fur women." At least this pair is well braced, and they are equipped with peep holes so you can check if they are available for occupancy. Twin outhouses were not unusual behind public buildings such as schools and churches or in cemeteries.

Photo courtesy Lambert Florin, author of Backyard Classics.

Need a Laxative? In Indiana

Life and signs can be baffling, confusing, and fun. Where would a more appropriate place be to advertise Feen-A-Mint Laxative than on this old outhouse located in the Pioneer Village at the Indiana State Fairgrounds? Outhouses were taken for granted as necessities, but now they are items of nostalgia. This one was moved in and sits by the area where many antique machines and historical farm equipment are demonstrated every day during the famous Indiana State Fair. Although many privies were routinely burned or torn down in earlier days, they are now frequently sold to the highest bidder.

Photo courtesy Purdue Ag Alumni.

CHAPTER 12
HUMOROUS SIGNS OF THE TIMES

The lighter side of a heavy subject. Could it really be true that before EPA was used as an acronym for the Environmental Protection Agency that it stood for Early Privy Action?

A Flush Beats a Full House in North Carolina

Does the sign mean what it says, or does it say the plumber knows that people enjoy humor? Other plumbers have created smiles with clever statements, including, "Do it yourself and then call us before it's too late," "Take us to your leaker," "If it wasn't for us plumbers, you wouldn't have no place to go," and "What if the plumbers convention was held in Flushing, New York?"

Photo by Walter Weber.

Need Your Bladder Flatter? In South Dakota

Simple words can be given a little humor. This sign is in the world's largest drug store, Wall Drug, Wall, South Dakota. In one case, a ladies' facility was identified with two words: "Patience and Fortitude." Patience is associated with solitaire. Fortitude is associated with strength to bear pain.

Photo by Walter Weber.

Flush in Kansas, the Sunflower State
(34th State, 1891)

It is only seven miles if you have time to go to Flush. You will see this sign giving you the directions to Flush when you are relatively close to Manhattan, Kansas. Flush was founded on August 24, 1854, and called Rock Creek until 1899. The church was built in 1866. In 1899, Henry J. Floersch, of German extraction, moved to town and applied to Washington to open a post office. In granting him a permit, the bureaucrats said that no one would be able to spell "Floersch" and so they sent the permit in the name of "Flush." And so there was a post office there of that name until 1927 when it was closed. The general store lasted until about a decade ago, reopened briefly as an antique store, and closed again. The church thrives and is known for its annual mid-summer picnic held in the basement. It is not true, however, that the weekly paper was known as *The Teepee.*

*Photo and information courtesy
Robin Higham, Editor,* Journal of the West, *Kansas State University.*

Bottoms Washed Free in West Virginia

Get to the bottom of the problem. Bottoms washed free on Sundays too, at this car wash in Charleston, West Virginia. Humor in signs is people humor.

Photo by Mark Weber.

This Out House is Not an Outhouse, in Utah

You are right when you see the big outhouse sign with an arrow, but you are wrong if you think it means what it says. This

was in Brigham, Utah. When I refueled my car, I asked the attendant about the unusual sign. He explained that it was a restaurant near the edge of the copper mining area.

Photo by Walter Weber.

Revival Salve in Pennsylvania

One definition of revival is renewed attention or interest. At least the billboard receives the tourists' attention, whether it revives the hemorrhoids or not.

Photo by Walter Weber.

Restrooms on Credit Cards? In Wyoming

What if you don't have a credit card? The sounds and sights on TV are all around us, but we are not aware of them until we tune in. Sometimes we can tune in on a sign and receive a misinterpreted interpretation. A credit card means, "Buy Now, Pray Later." It's called "Instant Credit," but it means "Instant Debt."

Photo by Walter Weber.

Toiletten in Hungary

This sign was at a roadside rest area in Hungary, close to the Austrian border. Even if you cannot read German, you could figure out the message. The men's side was identified with the same word, but the illustration showed a boy standing instead of sitting.

Photo courtesy Uniroyal.

Restrooms Behind Palm Trees in Hawaii, the Paradise of the Pacific (50th State, 1959)

If you use your imagination, you can visualize something other than what the sign indicates. This sign was at Pearl Harbor. The restrooms were behind the palm trees. It was interesting to note that the restrooms on the big island of Hawaii were all modern, but they did not have roofs.

Photo by Walter Weber.

There Is a Reason in Hawaii

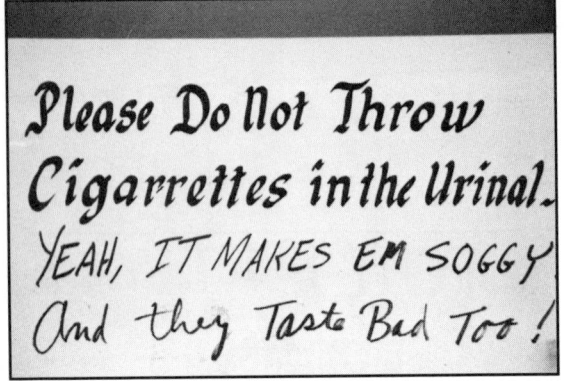

"Please do not throw cigarettes in the urinal." It was a sincere effort to avoid an unpleasant sanitation service. Two fellows added their graffiti to justify the request. From South Point, Hawaii, the southernmost village in the United States.

Photo by Walter Weber.

NO P C ME in Indiana

This license plate expresses the humor in Dr. Marks, a well-respected urologist in Lafayette, Indiana. A doctor in Colorado was suddenly swamped with a problem, the symptoms of which were not described in the medical books. It seemed to be an epidemic. There was no rash, no pruritus, no fever, no redness,

no pustules, but there was a serious discoloration of the posterior. After checking the many patients, the good doctor had apparently discovered a new variety of "black bottom." The cause was placed on recycling the local newspaper in the outhouse. The printer had received a batch of defective, improperly drying ink.

Photo by Walter Weber.

The Pause that Refreshes in Indiana

"And they said Coca Cola was the pause that refreshes." In a way, that sign is true. It just takes someone to adopt a famous slogan to a different meaning.

Photo by Walter Weber.

MEN Around the Corner in Indiana

The directions to the appropriate facilities are shown above an entrance to the Fine Arts Building at the Indiana State Fair. Facilities are offered for one of man's and woman's most basic needs.

Photo by Walter Weber.

Sewer Water Available in Indiana

Does that sign really mean that you will receive sewer water if you buy this vacant lot? That is one way to misinterpret this sign near the south edge of Indianapolis.

Photo by Walter Weber.

Equal Opportunity in Indiana

An equal opportunity bathroom for boys or girls still has restrictions limiting its occupancy. A practical application of this occurred in a restaurant in Pietown, New Mexico, which had a men's restroom and a ladies' restroom. Now the restaurant has only one. The manager told us that a government inspector determined the original kitchen was too small, so they had to remodel and finish with one larger restroom. Maybe they could call it "Us" or "Them." One mother put up a sign, "Please knock. This is an equal opportunity bathroom."

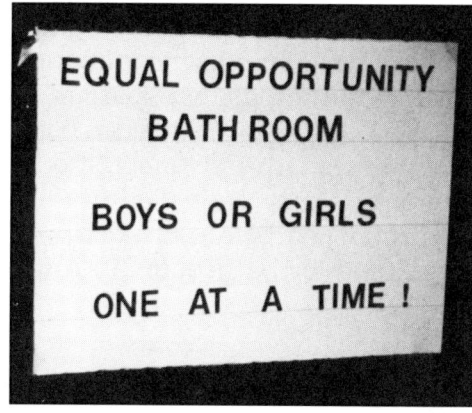

Photo by Walter Weber

Happiness Is to Get Here on Time in Indiana

Happiness is getting to the bathroom on time. People don't always go to the bathroom to bathe. Credit for inventing the flush toilet has long been given to the legendary Thomas Crapper. It has been reported that the fictitious Thomas Crapper was a brainchild of a British humorist who placed Crapper's birth in Throne, England, in 1837. An early version of flushing had been developed in the late fifteen hundreds by Queen Elizabeth's godson Sir John Har-

rington, who used an elevated water supply with gravity and valves, but there was no means of preventing return of unfragrant aromas. Could that have been a royal flush? The real forerunner of modern commodes was British watchmaker Alexander Cummings, who patented his idea in 1775. He used a U-shaped soil pipe under the commode to hold enough water to prevent the adverse effect of odiferous unfragrance on one's olfactory organs. He called it a stink trap. More than a hundred years passed before the flush toilet became a standard part of many indoor bathrooms in America.

Photo by Walter Weber.

Sales Tax on Restrooms in Indiana

This sign was in front of a service station in Lafayette, Indiana, the home of Purdue University. It looks like the service station manager was using humor power. Free speech may not be free. It is taxed.

Photo courtesy Fred Warren, Purdue University.

Happiness Is an Extra Roll of Toilet Paper in Indiana

Happiness is an extra roll of toilet paper on many occasions. The earliest attempt to introduce toilet paper was unsuccessful. It was first made available in packages of 500 individual sheets in 1857. The product was not readily accepted, probably because of the economy in using discarded newspapers or old catalogs, and the new product was basically discontinued. The first efforts at selling rolls of toilet paper were in Britain in 1879, but sales were slow. The first successful manufacture of toilet tissue in the United States was by Scotts. Happiness is not the absence of problems and difficulties. Happiness is successfully solving problems and overcoming difficulties.

Photo by Walter Weber.

Please Seat Yourself in Indiana

You do not have to wait for someone to seat you. This unintentional conclusion can be seen if you are sitting close to the entrance as you are enjoying a delicious pie or other tasty food in this gourmet restaurant. You won't have to look further if you are a lady who "wants to powder her nose." There is a companion to this picture.

Photo by Walter Weber.

Please Wait to Be Seated in Indiana

This is the reverse side of the "Seat Yourself" sign. You will see this view when sitting at one of the tables close to the entrance of an Indianapolis restaurant known for its outstanding pies, baked in their own oven. The polite statement, "I need to wash my hands," is often heard from men as they head for the restroom. This could be classified as a misinterpretable interpretation.

Photo by Walter Weber.

Old Commodes for Junk Mail in Indiana

Have you considered asking your mail carrier to separate your mail? Don't throw away that old commode when you modernize your bathroom. It is usable for junk mail. A study has been reported, indicating that a person spends eight months of his life opening junk mail.

Photo by Walter Weber.

CHAPTER 13
PRIVIA TRIVIA

The nice thing about trivia is that it keeps a person from worrying about important things. Many poems, songs, and comments have been made about the necessary house. Here are a few examples:

Ring Around the Seat

From *Passing of the Outhouse,* by Tom Murray

> My wife was very clean and neat
> So she buy paint for toilet seat.
> And one whole week we watch wid eye,
> But goldarn paint she no dry!
>
> My wife ain't tall, she kinda fat,
> Now you see just where she sat,
> She got big ring around complete
> Where she sat down on toilet seat.
>
> I say to her, "It serves you right,
> You try to be so goshdarn tight.
> Dat ten-cent paint, she ain't no good,
> she no dry on no darn wood!"
>
> My daughter too, get ring around
> When on da seat she do sit down.
> For wan whole week by gosh we wait
> and now we all got constipate.
>
> Wife's sister, her name Marie.
> She live all time in house wid me.
> Last night I look where she sat down,
> By gar, she too has ring around!

I try to wipe with turpentine,
She howl! like wolf . . . she lost her mind!
I'm scared lak heck for half a day,
Da skin come off, da paint she stay!

Now Mr. Woolworth, I ask you
Whaddoheck we gonna do?
For how can house be clean and neat
If paint no dry on toilet seat?

I live long time, but never see
A man what got so mad as me.
And when I think about your paint,
I get so mad, I almost faint!

Courtesy Tom Murray.

My friend, August Schwark, had a similar experience when he brought his new bride to his parents' home in 1945. His little brother had painted the interior of the outhouse. The paint failed to dry because he had not stirred it. The end result was that the new groom had to solve his bride's embarrassment by using turpentine to remove the fresh paint from her posterior.

The Passing of the Backhouse

By Charles T. Rankin, often attributed to James Whitcomb Riley (1849-1919), Indiana's most famous poet

When memory keeps me company
And moves to smiles the tears.
A weather-beaten object looms
Through the mist of years.
Behind the house and barn it stood
A half a mile or more
And hurrying feet a path had made
Straight to its swinging door.

Its architecture was a type
Of simple classic art
And in the tragedy of life
It played a leading part.
And oft the passing traveler
Drove slow and heaved a sigh
To see the modest hired girl
Slip out with glances shy.

We had a posey garden
That the women loved so well
I loved it, too, but better still
I loved the stronger smell
That filled the evening breezes
So full of homey cheer
And told the night-o'ertaken tramp
That human life was near.

On lazy August afternoons
It made a little bower
Delightful, where my grandsire sat
And whiled away an hour.
For there the summer morning
Its every cares entwined
And berry bushes reddened
In the steaming soil behind.

All day fat spiders spun their webs
To catch the buzzing flies
That flitted to and from the house
Where Ma was baking pies.
And once a swarm of hornets bold
Had built a palace there
And stung my unsuspecting Aunt–
I must not tell you where.

Then Father took a flaming pole–
That was a happy day–
He nearly burned the building up
But the hornets left to stay.

When summer's bloom began to fade
And winter to carouse,
We banked the little building
With a heap of hemlock boughs.

But when the crust was on the snow
And the sullen skies were grey,
In sooth the building was no place
Where one could wish to play.
We did our duties promptly there,
One purpose swayed the mind,
We tarried not, nor lingered long
On what was left behind.

The torture of that icy seat
Would make a spartan sob
For needs must scrape the goose-flesh
With a lacerating cob
That from a frost-encrusted nail
Was suspended by a string.
My Father was a frugal man
And wasted not a thing.

When Grandpa had to "go out-back"
To make his morning call,
We'd bundle up the dear old man
With a muffler and a shawl.
I knew the hole on which he sat–
'Twas padded all around–
And once I dared to sit there–
'Twas all too wide I found.

My loins were all too little
And I jack-knifed there to stay.
They had to come and get me out
Or I'd have passed away.
Then Father said ambition was
A thing that boys should shun,
And I must use the children's hole
'Til childhood days were done.

And still I marvel at the craft
That cut those holes so true,
The baby hole, and the slender hole
That fitted Sister Sue.
That dear old country landmark
I tramped around a bit,
And in the lap of luxury
My lot has been to sit.

But 'ere I die I'll eat the fruit
Of trees I robbed of yore,
Then seek the shanty where my name
Is carved upon the door.
I ween the old familiar smell
Will soothe my jaded soul;
I'm now a man, but none the less,
I'll try the other hole.

Outhouse Races Draw Big Crowds in South Dakota

Kadoka, South Dakota, is known for its famous Labor Day Outhouse Race. Crowds of viewers lined both sides of Kodoka's main street as the fourth annual South Dakota Championship Outhouse Race was run. The men's team set a new world's record in 1988 with their "Cactus Flats Flushless Wonder." The Powder Puff Division was won by the Kadoka Equity Union Exchange entry. Other entries included such original names as "Road Apple Express," "Midnight

Trots," "Kadoka Kleanest Krapper," "Buzzard Butte Biffy," "Ladder to Success," and "Pearson Basin Comfort Station." The proceeds are donated to the Kadoka Volunteer Fire Department.

Photo and information courtesy Matt Schofield, South Dakota correspondent; Clifford Parke, Kadoka Equity Union Exchange; and Joyce Hicks, Hilltop Hotel.

CHAPTER 14
PRIVY PRIVILEGES FOR PAMPERED PETS AND OTHER ANIMALS

Animals have their rights, too.

Privies for Pooches in Texas

Those old outhouses can still be used to bring a smile when a person stops for gasoline in Orlo, Texas. This one has a convenience door for dogs only. Many of the outhouses still seen have been converted into places to store garden tools.

Photo by Walter Weber.

Horses Just Can't Seem to Get the Knack of Toilet Training In South Carolina

Well-dressed horses wear diapers in Charleston, South Carolina. The city council passed an ordinance that required carriage operators to equip their horses or mules with adequate devices to prevent manure from falling on the streets of the city. The ordinance went into effect on February 1, 1978, and drew worldwide attention. These were not ordinary horses. These

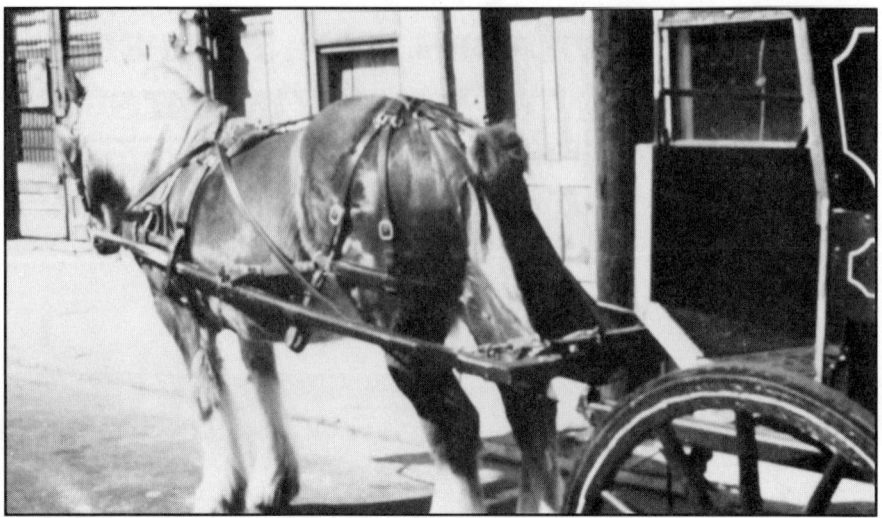

horses pulled the carriages that carried people through the historic district of Charleston. And these were not ordinary disposable diapers like those worn by people babies. The bags are attached to the harness and have a flap that covers the horse's posterior. (There is no evidence of diaper rash.) Maybe the diapers provide that fresh country-air feeling as they bring the special aroma closer to the guest.

Photo by Walter Weber.

Dogs Only in Kentucky

What about the other pets? It is said that after God created the world he made man and woman, and then to keep the whole thing from falling apart, he invented humor. This one was close to the highway.

Photo by Walter Weber.

Sex Discrimination for Pets in Ohio, the Buckeye State (17th State, 1803)

The thoughtful service station manager has provided equal facilities, using a little humor with his Pet Rest Area. The "his" part is equipped with an appropriate fire plug.

Photo by Walter Weber.

This Lawn Does Not Flush in Indiana

"This lawn does not flush, please empty your pets elsewhere." This person had a polite way of using humor to express his displeasure with uninvited dogs. One sign seen on a lawn read, "No Dogs in Here."

Photo by Walter Weber.

Used Oats Are Cheap in Florida, the Sunshine State
(27th State, 1845)

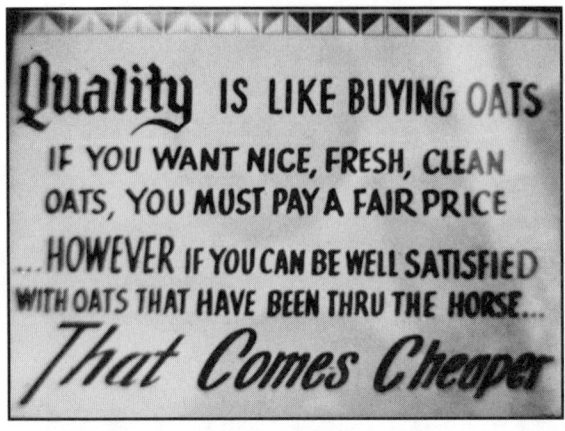

This sign was found at a flea market in West Palm Beach, Florida.

"Quality is like buying oats. If you want nice, fresh, clean oats, you must pay a fair price.... However if you can be well satisfied with oats that have been thru the horse . . . that comes cheaper."

Photo by Walter Weber.

Do Not Step on Exhaust in Indiana

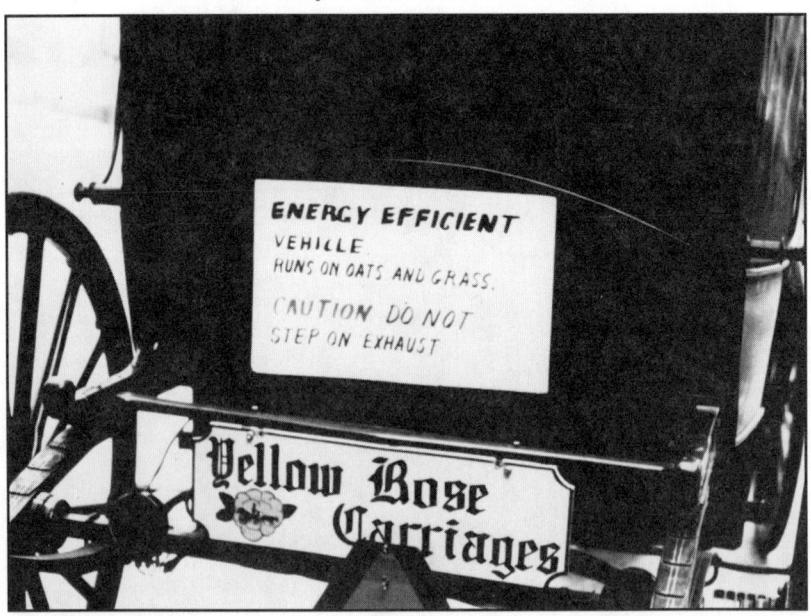

This energy-efficient vehicle runs on oats and grass. The caution sign exhorts one to not step on the exhaust. It was in 1840 when a horse was still the fastest transportation in the world.

Photo by Walter Weber.

Appendix

Fellow authors who have written interesting books involving outhouses and have kindly permitted me to use some of their material:

Lambert Florin, *Backyard Classics*, Superior Publishers, Seattle, Washington

Tom Murray, *Passing of the Outhouse*, 33 Mountain View Circle, Swan Lake, Mira Loma, California 91752

Bob Ross, *Muddled Meanderings in an Outhouse* (three versions), P.O. Box 927, Bozeman, Montana 59715

Norman D. Weis, *The Two Story Outhouse*, $12.95 plus $1.00 postage, The Caxton Printers, Ltd., Caldwell, Idaho 83605

Edward Chappel, *Looking at Buildings, Fresh Advices, A Research Supplement*, Vol. 5, No. 6, 1984

Ronald Barlow, *The Vanishing American Outhouse*, $15.95, Windmill Publishing, 2147 Windmill View Road, El Cajon, California 92020

ABOUT THE AUTHOR

Walter Weber is an entomologist by training, a photographer by hobby, a speaker and writer by choice. Walter invites you to his 100th birthday January 6, 2011. No gifts, please. Walter grew up on a farm near Melvin, Illinois. He is an alumnus of the University of Illinois, with a master's degree from Purdue University.

Walter spent twelve years teaching vocational agriculture, biology, and chemistry and thirty years with the Indiana Farm Bureau Cooperative, where he wrote their annual *Pest Control Guide*.

Walter and his wife Eunice have carried their camera to all fifty states and several foreign countries.

After retirement, Walter served as consultant to the Rid-A-Bird Company and E. I. DuPont Company. He has written three books on vector-borne pathogens: *Health Hazards from Pigeons, Starlings and English Sparrows; Diseases Transmitted by Rats and Mice;* and *Fleas, Ticks & Cockroaches, Disease Disseminators*. He has also written *Signs of Your Life*, a collection of signs expressing humor and fun, and is co-author of *Funny Bones: Health and Humor Experts*.

Walter is a member of the Indiana Academy of Science, the National Speakers Association, and the Lutheran Church. He is a Registered Professional Entomologist. He lives at 36 West Roberts Road, Indianapolis, Indiana 46217; his phone number is (317) 786-7251.